Carry on Farming

By the Same Author

The Benefits Racket
Down Among the Dossers
The Decline of an English Village
The Hunter and the Hunted
Weather-forecasting the Country Way
Cures and Remedies the Country Way
Animal Cures the Country Way
Weeds the Country Way
The Journal of a Country Parish
Journeys into Britain
The Country Way of Love
The Wildlife of the Royal Estates
A Fox's Tale
The Fox and the Orchid
Dust in a Dark Continent. (Africa)
Gardening the Country Way
A Peasant's Diary
Gone to the Dogs
Vocal Yokel

For Children
How the Fox got its Pointed Nose
How the Heron Got Long Legs.

Carry on Farming

Robin Page

EXCELLENT PRESS
LUDLOW

Excellent Press
7 Corve Street
Ludlow
Shropshire SY8 1DB

First published in the UK by Excellent Press 1999

Copyright © Robin Page 1999

A copy of the British Library Cataloguing in Publication Data for this
title is available from the British Library.

ISBN 1 900318 10 5

Printed in the United Kingdom

Dedication

———

I would like to dedicate *Carry on Farming* to all those friends and relations who took their leave of this planet during the period covered by this book. I still miss them enormously – they have gone, but the fight for their countryside and their Britain goes on, as demonstrated by all those who took part in the Countryside March.

Contents

Contents

Preface

Carry On Farming is another collection of my assorted rural writings. Sometime ago I was asked by a total stranger: 'How do you do it? It must be really difficult to make up all those stories so regularly'. I could hardly believe my ears; make up stories? There is so much going on in the British countryside that there is no need to make up anything.

Sadly the countryside is now in crisis; urban politicians are so out of touch that farming is experiencing its worst depression for seventy years; the Common Agricultural Policy has turned into a nightmare; the EU is now revealed as an undemocratic, centralised fiasco (every bit as undemocratic as the Europe under Hitler and Eastern Europe caught behind the Iron Curtain). The whole of our minority rural culture is under attack from the very people who claim to be in favour of 'multi-culturalism' and 'minority rights'.

Yet the heart of the countryside still beats proudly. This book covers a truly remarkable time – an election, the Countryside Rally, the Countryside March and crisis after crisis caused by cynical urban politicians and urban bureaucrats out of their depth.

For me this was also a time of many changes. I experienced great highs and lows, tears, laughter and losses that I could not have anticipated; the events that have made up my life could not have been foreseen by somebody writing rural fiction. But there have been gains too; as the Countryside Restoration Trust has continued to grow, so its message has become ever more relevant as the work of the bureaucrats and politicians have continued to wreak havoc to both farming and wildlife. I believe that the work of the CRT shows a way forward; the more people who join will also help to increase its voice and its effectiveness. Both will be needed in large measures if the current attacks on our countryside and rural life are to be repulsed.

For those wanting a living and working countryside – a countryside containing real people, good food, abundant wildlife and attractive landscapes, then please join The Countryside Restoration Trust as a matter of urgency – write to The CRT, Barton, Cambridgeshire, CB3 7AG for details.

I would like to thank the Editors of *The Daily Telegraph*, *The Field* and *Country Living* for permission to reproduce articles that have appeared in their esteemed organs; in *Carry on Farming* however, the material is all unexpurgated. Finally, I would like to thank Margaret Taylor for feeding all the material into her computer.

1

Holly Blues and Happy Elms

———

Suddenly spring has come. For me it has been a memorable few days, as it has thrown me once more into the middle of a great wildlife mystery. A few years ago I wrote that the beautiful holly blue butterfly had become extinct locally. I mourned its loss and blamed pollution, the weather and development; then, to emphasise the breadth and depth of my knowledge the butterfly re-appeared. Six or seven years ago during April and May there was almost a glut of them; everywhere I glanced there seemed to be not one holly blue, but two or three. Then, in the early Nineties they vanished again, from abundance to none in just a year.

Now suddenly they are back. I noticed them as I was passing some ivy covered elm stumps in a neighbour's garden. At first I thought some petals of plum blossom had blown into the ivy, then wings opened and the sun caught a tiny patch of deep-sea blue among the dark green leaves. Five pristine holly blues had just emerged; this strange, unpredictable butterfly had reappeared for a second time.

In any event the holly blue is an unusual butterfly. There are two generations each year; in the spring the females usually lay their eggs on holly leaves, hence the name 'holly blue', but in the autumn they lay on ivy, which explains why these butterflies had suddenly appeared in my neighbour's hedge. However, it fails to explain why the species is not called the 'holly and the ivy blue'.

But although the butterfly is back, the mystery remains; why does the population of the holly blue keep rising and crashing? Various 'experts' have no idea what happens and these include Robert Goodden, Director of Worldlife at Sherborne, who has studied most species of British butterfly. The other oddity is that when the population crashes, the recovery must be based on brothers and sisters breeding; so why doesn't in-breeding cause a problem? Whatever their private lives I'm glad to have them back and hope that the next crash is many years away.

The riddle of the holly blue butterfly reminds me of another mystery that I simply cannot explain. Dutch Elm Disease ravaged my parish several years ago and as soon as any remaining suckers begin to get a reasonable height, the dreaded disease suddenly hits them too. It is a tragedy, as the elm was such an important feature of this part of lowland England; it was important for the landscape and it was important for wildlife too. Yet every now and again that old familiar shape can still be seen; I realised this about three years ago when it suddenly dawned on me that a tree my subconscious called an oak, about four miles away, was in fact a giant roadside elm. It was, and still is, in perfect condition and I was amazed.

Then four more were pointed out to me along a country road close to Therfield, near Royston, again, all in apparently perfect health. They have not been injected with insecticide; they are not fancy hybrids and they look completely normal and natural – but somehow they have managed to stay alive. So why have they managed to survive, when all their neighbours succumbed years ago?

The other question that needs to be asked is why, if there have been genuine survivors, has English Nature not taken cuttings to see how they survived? If they are indeed Dutch Elm Disease resistant, then English Nature should have already found out whether their suckers, or even their seeds, are immune, and if they are, they should have been replanting these disease free elms by the thousand. The question of elm seeds is another part of the mystery; some experts claim that the natural germination of seeds has not taken place in this country for 200 years, yet the trees in the elm woods and spinneys of my childhood were producing so many seeds it would have been impossible to count them.

Fortunately David Bellamy, is now doing what the conservation quangos should have done long ago; he is calling for information on mature, healthy elms. He wants their location, their variety – English Elm or Wych Elm, and a couple of large leaves, with stalks, pressed between sheets of newspaper. Who knows, this could be the start of an exciting development to bring the elm back to Britain. It is a wonderful thought, as the elm dominated the landscape of so much of lowland England. It is strange too, that even after all these years I still miss the elm. One of the reasons that I love visiting the Isles of Scilly is that on the main island, St Mary's, it is still possible to walk through a small wood of healthy elms.

By coincidence next weekend sees the start of 'Walk in the Woods', or more accurately the 'Esso Walk in the Woods' campaign. It is an idea to get people to visit woods; presumably the visitors are expected to drive to a wood in Esso fuelled vehicles, so that the trees can then absorb the extra airborne CO_2. Amazingly a Mori survey carried out for 'Esso Walk in the Woods' reveals that 30% of our strange population have never visited a wood and that only a paltry 14% admit to have spoken to a tree. I talk to trees regularly; I find them far less dense than politicians. However, I have to confess that I am not yet one of the 3% who claims to have kissed a tree; but even that could change the next time I find a large, mature disease free elm.

2

Pikes and Ducks

────

I have always had a strange love/hate relationship with pike, as I have with several other of our meaner predators. Whenever I see a pike I always marvel at its streamlined, menacing beauty, but as soon as I see a small fish taken, or notice the new mallard ducklings disappearing one by one, I feel angry and irritated. As a boy I would vent my anger by pelting them with stones. On sunny days I would even hunt them with an air rifle. Thankfully for the pike the wonders of 'refraction' meant that all my efforts at revenge were wasted.

Recently a largish pike appeared in the brook. It arrived after a heavy downpour just as the Environment Agency had finished its repair work. The water level rose, and then, when it fell away the pike was lurking on the edge of a deep pool created by the EA. I assume it had swum upstream during the spate and had found the pool ideal for mugging unsuspecting smaller fish.

Last Sunday morning I saw the pike again at very close quarters – so close that I could pick its head up and touch its needle-like teeth. Yes, the pike had received its cum-uppance and become an otter's Saturday night supper, with the left-overs abandoned on the bank. A menacing predator had been eaten by a cuddly predator, and it couldn't have happened to a more deserving, anti-social specimen.

I was pleased to see the evidence of the otters' return as they had been absent for two months following the disturbance caused by the EA's activities. Their presence was confirmed again by four fresh 'spraints' (droppings) under one of the road bridges. Since the otters returned to our little brook three years ago, several spraints have been analysed to see what the depositors had been eating. Surprisingly many pike scales have been identified, suggesting that pike form a large percentage of the otters' local diet. Yet the pike is so fast off the mark I had always assumed that it would be too fast for an otter. It means that either the otter has an astonishing turn of speed, or that the pike has no stamina and quickly slows.

One of the results of the otter's liking for pike has already shown itself. Not only are there fewer pike, but the numbers of other smaller coarse fish such as dace, roach and chub appear to have increased enormously as one of their main predators has been removed. Of course in the long term this will help the otters too as more young coarse fish will grow into large old fish. I had better stop this, I can feel a PhD coming on.

The cold wind of the 'blackthorn winter' has made cricket

watching difficult. Cricket is one of my weaknesses and virtually the only benefit we locals get from living on the doorstep of Cambridge University is that we get free First Class cricket. More to the point, the University Cricket Club is one of the few University organisations that allows local peasants like me to join. Being a member means that on a bitterly cold day I can watch cricket in the warmth and comfort of the Fenners pavilion.

This year the cricket has been made more interesting by the appointment of one of my cricketing heroes as the University coach – Derek Randall, the old England and Notts player. His humour and enthusiasm is already showing itself. At a recent match when cover dropped what should have been a reasonably easy catch, Randall immediately appeared at the trot, to present the offending fielder with a large blue bucket. One of the funniest stories about him occurred when he was touring India with England. At a posh reception he tasted caviare for the first time; his reaction was interesting: 'This blackcurrant jam tastes of fish to me'.

The sad thing about the present University team is that it is made up almost entirely of public school boys. Sadly, at state schools cricket no longer appears to be on the syllabus. Teachers claim that they have no time; I suppose the truth is that many of today's teachers are too lazy to take classes after 4 o'clock. If public school teachers can make the time, why can't teachers at state schools?

The consequences of cricket disappearing from state schools is not just seen at universities, but in ordinary village cricket too. The supply of young players coming into village cricket is drying up simply because the schools have ceased to teach and play it. As a result most of my local village teams are all gradually becoming geriatric and I am about to start my tenth consecutive 'final season'. I have to keep playing as so few young players are coming through to allow me to retire. By slowly removing cricket from our rural culture teachers have a lot to answer for. The problems started during the 'teachers' strikes' of a few years ago. I was a school governor at the time. In my humble view laziness was excused as 'political action'. School cricket has never recovered.

In my last chapter I mentioned sensible people like me who actually talk to trees, and also those rather strange people who admit to kissing trees. Now David Bellamy has contacted me about hugging trees and elm trees in particular. He says that he is only interested in mature elms with a 'huggable trunk, i.e. a circumference of more than two metres' – I think he means an elm tree with a circumference of more than six feet or two yards. So information concerning healthy' huggable elms to The Conservation Foundation, 1 Kensington Gore, London SW7 2AR. Information about kissable elms and talkative elms, please keep to yourselves.

3

Verging on Disaster

———

The suburbanisation of the countryside continues apace. What makes things even more worrying for me is that my local countryside is not only being suburbanised, but also sanitised and homogenised.

A few years ago the rampant roadside verge cutters were persuaded not to cut quite so enthusiastically. It was wasted breath; this year Cambridgeshire County Council's assorted cutters, mowers and slashers are back at their worst. Incredibly, grass cutting began before the grass had actually started growing. Now that the grass is growing they seem to be in their element.

Verges where road safety and visibility are not an issue have been turned into imitation lawns and the parish's only cowslip verge has been flattened while the cowslips were in full bloom. The cowslip verge is an interesting one. Last year the cowslips were ruined as a cycle track was put down through them. Now the survivors have been cut in their prime. The design of the cycleway puzzled me; it passed through the middle of the verge, instead of following the bend on the inside. Now all has been revealed; the inside of the bend was planted with hundreds of daffodils. So an attractive, almost wild bend has become tame, looking neat, tidy and suburban.

Just down the road where a new roundabout has been constructed near the M11 we have had thousands more daffodils planted, not the golden daffodils of Wordsworth, but sickly, mutated pale daffodils of the garden centre. When I saw the workman busy planting things I had foolishly thought that a wildflower verge was being created. I should have known better; some small minded suburban planner had decided to impose his twee little world onto the general countryside and those of us who live and work in it. A quarter of mile further on another potential large wild roundabout has been mown like a lawn. It could have been left wild for butterflies and skylarks – instead the Council is spending its time and our money turning it into a bowling green. I thought local authorities were supposed to have no spare money!

Verges and roundabouts with cowslips and wildflowers would look natural and require minimum maintenance. Daffodils and lawn mowing require maximum maintenance. Amusingly Cambridgeshire County Council boasts that it consults 'the people'. I have met nobody who has been consulted by the Council's Phantom Daffodil Planting Department. The best thing the County Council can do now is to offer people free bulb digging. Tame daffodils should be in tame gardens, not the almost open countryside.

Our Lib/Dem county councillor came to a local Parish Council meeting recently – not consulting, but apologising. With his tail between his legs he told us how sorry he was that due to financial cuts (presumably with the exception of the Daffodil Planting Department) seventeen of the parish's street lights were to be cut off. Soon he was flabbergasted; a majority of the council complained that seventeen lights were not enough and would the CC switch off many more.

It is astonishing how many people who now live in the country become neurotic at the thought of losing street lights. I can understand old people wanting lights, again out of irrational fear, but what is the point of spending millions of pounds on lights, powered by non-renewable energy, lighting deserted roads at three o'clock in the morning? Interestingly villages without street lights are said to have lower crime and accident rates than villages with lights. Presumably muggers and robbers can operate better when they can see who they are mugging and where they can break-in. I hope one of the street lights dimmed in my parish is the revolting orange monstrosity outside my house – give me the stars and moonbeams any day.

I have just renewed my passport and was appalled at the small shoddy imitation that has arrived back as my Euro-passport. It would appear that even passports have been sanitised and homogenised. It is ghastly, it looks like a Spanish dog licence. Because of my alarm I have had to send away for an old looka-like British Passport cover, to hide the Euro-imposter.

At first glance it looks similar to the old passport, but there have been one or two subtle changes because of Crown Copyright. At the bottom of the coat of arms, Latin has replaced French, and translated it reads 'Long Live the Corgis'. The other Latin inscription says 'Who wants to be a European Anyway'. In the coat of arms we find a British bulldog, the Union Jack, a pint of beer and a cricket bat. I am going to Spain for a few days soon – I shall be carrying my new British passport with pride. These excellent passport covers can be obtained from Opal Options, PO Box 432, Reading, RG4 8FY – telephone 01189479573.

Oh dear, I have been dreaming again. The last action dream involved trying to run John Gummer out at cricket and throwing my cup of tea over my trousers as I dozed in my armchair. I was dozing in the armchair again the other day when I thought I was picking up the egg bucket. Two large rats jumped out and I took a tremendous kick at one, kicking Bramble completely off his bean bag as he dozed in front of me. Down the road at the farm-house my elderly father has done even better; he was apparently driving the tractor and trailer downhill and fell out of bed. Interpretations on postcards only please.

8

4

Bees and Beef

———

Following my last Chapter a reader has sent me a cutting from his local paper. It demonstrates yet again how the people of these urbanised isles are becoming divorced from nature. Behold, a swarm of honey bees decided to 'hang out' in a tree in the very centre of that sprawling blot known as Milton Keynes. So how did those wonderful new-town burgers cope with this common summer occurrence? First of all the police sealed off the area and then, according to the local paper, the 'Bee-Busters' were called: 'Kitted up in full protective gear, a pest officer BRAVELY went where no one else dare'. And what did the 'brave Bee-Buster' do? Why, he sprayed the bees with poison, of course, killing the entire swarm. A spokesman was proud of his Council's achievement: 'We usually charge up to £32.50 to treat a bees' nest. We treated this as an emergency and no charge will be made on this occasion'. What the great saviours of Milton Keynes should be told is that the swarm was a threat to nobody; the average bee-keeper could have collected the whole swarm, alive, in a cardboard box, wearing little protection, and the bees should now be busy making honey in a domestic hive. Killing the entire swarm was nothing less than a piece of urban vandalism.

It is a good month for vandalism. Now comes a story of yet more irresponsibility from that centre for agricultural madness – MAFF. The other day I had the good fortune to travel to Hertfordshire to see a wonderful herd of British Longhorn cattle. They are superb beasts; despite their long horns they are placid, they eat virtually anything, including thistles and nettles, and because of their character and diet Hertfordshire County Council are using them to stop scrub encroachment on areas of wet common land.

Not only are the Longhorns attractive to look at, they also make very good beef. They are slow to mature and so the meat is firm, lean and full of taste – everything that the average young, fast fed, rubbery, tasteless supermarket joint is not. The herd is owned by Bob Williams and the cattle are his pride and joy. The herd is virtually organic, and because of the way he looks after them and feeds them they are BSE free. 'Look at those beautiful bullocks,' he said, pointing to his young stock; they were indeed a fine sight. 'They usually end up in the butcher's shop at about three years – that means I am now simply breeding them to burn; it's disgusting'. He was right; it is disgusting – it is yet more vandalism based on ignorance, thanks to the EU, Mr. Hogg and the wonderful Mr. Dorrell. This great trinity decreed that all cattle killed over 30 months old must be incinerated because of BSE. The great intellectuals have yet to tell us how burning BSE free animals saves us from BSE. It can surely only be a matter of time before Messrs Hogg and Dorrell receive knighthoods.

Because of this nonsense, all Bob's beef cattle will be burnt. I know that they cannot have BSE; Bob Williams knows they haven't got BSE and even in his quieter moments, the inept Mr. Hogg must surely know that they have no problem with BSE – yet they must be burnt, simply to increase Britain's cull numbers to impress the equally ignorant European Beefocrats.

Astonishingly, at the same time that BSE free cattle are still being slaughtered, calves from BSE proven parents are being allowed to live. It is a logic that defies description. But nothing should surprise us now; MAFF has just informed the world that it is carrying out no research into the effects of eating meat full of antibiotics (broiler hens in particular – good healthy white meat – allegedly); the fact that it could be lowering our resistance to disease is apparently of no concern. Watch this space, this year, next year or some time in the not too distant future.

The CRT hay meadow has been wonderful this year. Full of flowers, bees and butterflies. The butterflies have been outstanding – clouds of common blue, brown argus, small copper, painted lady, etc. It has been astonishing to see people pull up on the road nearby and look in wonder – at wildflowers. Who would have thought it two generations ago – stopping to look at wildflowers;

then every verge, driftway and hay meadow had them in profusion.

On a recent trip to the Basque country I was amazed to see hay meadows almost identical to the one we are trying to create. I suppose the Common Agricultural Policy will soon put paid to them. Every roadside verge and every meadow was full of colour, wings and the sound of insects. But there was more too. There seemed to be a nightingale in almost every bush and the red-backed shrike was common. A few years ago I ventured into Thetford Forest to see Britain's last breeding red-backed shrike, the 'butcher bird' – the damage we have done to our wildlife over recent years is almost beyond belief.

I was in Spain with a number of twitchers – sorry, birders – including one of Britain's hottest spotters, David Tomlinson. He runs an organisation called Gourmet Birds. He assures me that he does not eat each bird after he has watched it. On the last day we were up to 99 species – the birders wanted 100 and had heard of purple sandpipers near a harbour wall. This meant birders, bins, telescopes and tripods clambering over lines of semi-naked sunbathing Spanish ladies, as we tried to get to a point over-looking the birds. It is the first time I have ever climbed over a naked woman to get to a purple sandpiper.

5

Good News and Bad

We are again in the middle of the agricultural show season and as a result I have some good news and some bad. The good news is that I have at last found a show worse than the Royal. The bad news is that it is the one on my own doorstep, the East of England Show. If any foreigners, or visitors from another planet had dropped in this year, they would have been excused for thinking that the primary product of British farms was teddy bears. Why or how so many teddy bears should be on sale at an agricultural show is totally beyond me. The other peculiarity of the show was the number of radio station stands, all blaring out their pounding beat music. Consequently not only does the East of England Show no longer look like an agricultural show, but it does not sound like one either.

The show summed up well the view of the East Anglia farming establishment towards conservation. The Conservation tent was erected in the far north eastern corner of the showground, tight up against the boundary fence. Consequently those people manning the displays, representing the CPRE, FWAG, CRT and the Wildfowl Trust had plenty of time for peace and quiet; farmers inside the tent were almost as rare as honey bees in Milton Keynes.

The day after my visit I was approached by a farmer who had wanted to visit the CRT display but had failed to find it. The 'Information' point could give him no information whatsoever and he was not amused. He is a working farmer, with a small farm and much wildlife, the sort who no longer seem to be represented by the farming establishment. I suppose I should not have been surprised by the show's lack of conservation interest. The landscape and wildlife devastation in East Anglia has not been caused by urban incomers, planners, or developers, it has been caused by many of the farmers and landowners themselves – the very people who claim to be countrymen. It is bizarre.

A peculiar story comes to me from the Rare Breeds Survival Trust about an agricultural show close to Gloucester. The RBST had a large Greyfaced Dartmoor ram on its stand which obviously impressed a passer-by. She walked up to look at the beast and was given a potted history of the breed. She was not impressed: 'No, I don't want all that,' she interrupted, 'is it a pig, a sheep or a cow?' This tale, is, astonishingly, perfectly true.

My purpose for going to the East of England Show was to visit the Peterborough Royal Foxhound Show. It is the most important hound show of the year and Anglia television wanted me to go

12

and have a look. I had never been to a hound show before and so I had to dress for the part, which meant wearing my late grand-father's seventy-year-old bowler hat. I looked a magnificent sight, but unfortunately not all those present agreed. One of the first people I bumped into, and at his size a collision could not have been avoided, took one look at me and burst into raucous laughter, threatening at the same time to jump on my magnifi-cent hat. It was most uncalled for, but what can you expect from my colleague Mr R. W. F. Poole?

I remember meeting a man several years ago who claimed to be called Mr R. W. F. Poole. He said he was following the 'Hay diet' and from his slimline waist he could have put several brace of ferrets down his trousers. This Mr Poole would have found it difficult to accommodate one young weasel, yet alone a ferret. To put it in the hunting terms he loves so much, the Hay diet appeared to have 'gone away', replaced by what I wonder – the chocolate eclair diet, or the strawberries and cream diet – only time, or a solicitor's letter will tell. Next time I venture north I shall check to see if there are in fact two Mr Pooles or just one. The hound show itself was fascinating. Hounds are most attrac-tive, friendly dogs and there were assembled the best hounds from thirty of the country's leading packs. But they were also working dogs, proper dogs, and so the whole thing had little in common with Crufts. There the dogs seem to have become little more than living ornaments.

Those visiting the hound show were a complete cross-section and the variety of accents, from plum-filled Eton to R-rolling Cotswolds, confirmed the range of interest. Again it seemed incredible that these dogs and these people should arouse so much anger from so many people who know so little about them. Just as that woman in Gloucester did not know the difference between a cow, sheep and pig, so many people who have never seen a fox, a hound or a hunt actually have an opinion about hunting and the long traditions that go with it. Interestingly one of the most common arguments against hunting these days claims that 'the vast majority of British people want to ban hunting and so it is only democratic to ban it'.

This is interesting. I have not met one person yet who believed that MPs, deserved, earned, or should have received their recent 26% pay rise. Yet a large majority of MPs voted for greed rather than democracy; this large proportion of MPs included several who argue for the will of the majority on hunting. Of course they will have a good reason for defending their actions – those who indulge in humbug and hypocrisy always do.

6

Bill and Ben

There is one golden rule in the summer countryside that should be followed at all times. If you find a young animal or bird apparently deserted, leave it alone; the parents are usually just around the corner, and if they're not, then nature will quickly take its course. It is a rule that I have chosen to ignore for years. Consequently at various times I have fostered pheasants, rabbits, foxes, a tawny owl, jackdaws, a kestrel, etc etc. Some interventions are successful, others have led to disaster and sorrow.

This year it was badger cubs. The message awaiting me one afternoon was that there were three badger cubs behaving oddly in a neighbour's wheat. They were above ground at mid-day, when they should have been underground, and they were about a quarter of a mile from the nearest sett. It was very strange.

By the time I arrived on the scene there were only two to be found. They were curled up, almost in balls in the crop, miserable and frightened. They muttered a few phrases of disagreement, when I picked them up – they did not feel very fat, but they did not seem to be starving either. I was puzzled and telephoned Ruth Murray, the 'badger lady' of Dartmoor. After retiring from farming Ruth's main interest has been badgers and over the years she has saved hundreds of orphaned, threatened and injured animals.

In her view, the behaviour of the young cubs was so strange that she felt the sow had gone absent and they were hungry and were looking for her. Almost inevitably, she believed, the mother had been hit by a car or snared; if the cubs were taken in they stood a chance; if they were left they would almost certainly die. This gave me no real choice, I had to take them in. Out came the lamb feeding bottle and after a quick trip to get some milk powder, for puppies, my transformation into a badger's foster-mother began. We combed the wheat for the third cub but it had disappeared. Earlier in the day my nephew had seen an enquiring fox near the cubs – whether the fox had taken the missing cub I have no idea.

The first day was a problem; Bill and Ben hated being touched and would not suck. Fortunately I only got bitten once, but soon Ben was sucking well, and Bill took to licking the leaking teat so quickly that his tongue must have ached. Then disaster almost struck; Ben reacted against his food, leading to more frantic phone-calls to Ruth Murray to put him right.

Gradually the cubs began to respond. Their heads and ears would react when I called them and they began to lap from a saucer. I decided it was time to start weaning them. They looked healthy and in the long term it seemed as if the story was going to have a happy ending. After a week, I arrived in the stable at six in the morning for the early feed – it was empty. I could not believe my eyes. I had blocked a drain in the old building to prevent just this. Then I saw it; a low hole in the wall between the stable and the old raised granary (a listed building) next door. The cubs had got out of the stable under the granary and away. I was mortified; I had fed them well for a week, simply to give them enough energy to escape.

I made a search of all the buildings and the fields immediately surrounding the farm, but with all the vegetation at its full summer height it was impossible. At dusk I searched again; walking around the edges of the fields, looking, listening and hoping. That night I left the stable door open; but I never saw them again and the stable remained empty.

With luck they might just have survived. The week of feeding may have enabled them to wean on beetles and bugs and there are numerous places for them to find shelter and shade at this time of year. But then, too their luck may have run out; they may have met a fox, a dog, or even a large boar badger; they could have wandered onto a road and perhaps they could not cope without milk and slowly starved to death.

It was both a pleasure and an education to look after Bill and Ben, even though I had them only a week. Their departure was unexpected and sad, but I am glad that once again I had broken summer's golden rule. At times nature really does need a hand, even if it sometimes ends in failure and sorrow.

For years we had few badgers in the parish and strangely, the largest sett was right next to a rifle range. Over recent years the badger population has exploded and I now know of half a dozen setts. Similar stories come from all over the country. Yet many people still believe the badger to be 'rare' and 'endangered' whereas in reality it is one of our most common animals.

To me the misconceptions about badger numbers are another indication that people are simply not going into the countryside as they did in the past, and once there they do not recognise the signs and tracks around them. Even 'country' children no longer understand the natural things around them. Recently a school from the edge of the Fens visited the CRT land. As I was showing the class the artificial otter holt that has been erected I said it was for 'a rare, furry animal that had just come back to the area. It lives mainly in the water and eats fish. What is it?' A ten year old boy put his hand up and answered quite seriously: 'A hedgehog'.

A local farmer has an even better story. While on a school visit to his pigstyes a little boy was excited at the sight of eight piglets sucking from a sow. Suddenly he shouted to a friend: 'Come and see this, there are eight little pigs blowing-up a big one'.

7

The Hedgerow Harvest

The season is changing and autumn approaches. I love the change and I do not have to look for flocks of migrating birds, or worsening weather to see it. I look first in the hedgerows, for there the change can be seen at its earliest.

It is a gentle change, slow and subtle. The summer hedge gradually becomes the ripening and fruiting hedge, when the natural harvest of the hedgerow allows bird, bee, butterfly and animal to build up their reserves for the hardships, or long deep sleep, of winter.

The natural hedgerow harvest is rich and varied and each new crop gives a different flavour and colour. There are nuts, berries and fruits to satisfy the appetites of all those wanting to feed. There are blackberries, sloes – the bitter fruit of the blackthorn, hips, haws, hops, hazel and beech nuts, crab apples, wild pear, the dark berries of buckthorn, dog wood and ivy. There are conkers, walnuts and sometimes wild plums and cherries. There are bright berries too, bryony, holly and spindle making a wonderful collection and variety of colours and tastes.

I have to confess that sometimes I try to share the natural harvest with the wildlife, or, more accurately I attempt to beat them to it. My favourites are wild blackberries; they seem to develop a rich bitter-sweet flavour that garden blackberries can never match. I have competition for them of course. Thrushes and blackbirds love them and as 'ripeness' turns to 'over-ripeness', the butterflies arrive for their share of the sugary juice. The red admirals and the commas are the greatest lovers of the old fruit and they are often followed by the peacocks and small tortoiseshells. It is one of the oddities of the blackberry plant that it will often have

17

both fruit and blossom at the same time, when the attractive gate-keeper will choose the blossom and the réd admiral the fruit.

But others eat blackberries too if they get the chance. Last year as I was filling my basket, as I love both blackberry and apple pie and blackberry jam, a wood mouse appeared near my right hand. I was as startled as it was. Lower down, near the ground, the fruit is often picked well before I arrive on the scene. It is easy to spot those responsible, as the droppings of foxes suddenly begin to contain many blackberry pips, as well as numerous plum stones, cherry pips and the wings of black beetles. I suspect that others also like the low fruit, particularly hedgehogs and badgers, although not at the same time – the poor hedgehog is often included on the badger's diet.

My other favourite fruit is the sloe. Despite its bitter taste when bitten raw – a taste that it is so awful that the fruit is impossible to swallow – when soaked in a solution of sugar and gin it makes a welcome, warming drink for winter. I have to confess that it is my favourite tipple for a cold winter and my excuse is that it also helps to fight off colds.

Others obviously share my views about the bitter taste of the natural berry as sloes are one of the last berries to be eaten. They usually hang around until well into winter when hunger makes matters of taste irrelevant. I have always wondered whether birds can taste, as they seem to swallow berries whole. But the hips and haws seem to go well before the sloes.

The other wild fruit that I like is the hazel nut. Unfortunately I never arrive in time for them as the grey squirrels usually strip the trees and bushes of nuts well before they are ripe. I suppose their anxiety to strip the hedge is a mixture of hunger, greed and a desire to lay down a winter larder as quickly as possible. The grey squirrel always looks so attractive as it collects nuts and buries them here, there and everywhere; it is such a shame that this import from America should cause so much damage to young birds and eggs in the spring, and also that it should have played such a major role in the demise of our indigenous red squirrel.

The charming dormouse does things slightly differently from

the squirrel. It too likes hazel nuts, but stores them as a layer of fat. It needs this in order to get it through the winter during its underground hibernation.

In several of the older hedges around my parish there are walnut trees. Again walnuts are popular with both man and beast. I am not a great lover of raw walnuts, usually eaten with salt in these parts, but I love pickled walnuts. That is another winter delight – warm, new bread, a piece of mature cheddar cheese and pickled walnuts – followed, on medicinal grounds, by a nip of sloe gin.

Rooks, crows and magpies are great pickers and robbers of walnuts. Often I have seen birds mobbed by others all for the sake of a nut. Sometimes the prize is dropped and I have found walnuts in the middle of fields at least half a mile from the nearest tree. But even then the fallen walnut will not be wasted; again, I have found walnuts hidden under straw bales by 'field mice' (wood mice), many hundreds of yards from the nearest tree. I do not believe even the mightiest mouse could drag, push or carry a walnut that far. The only explanation is that a bird dropped it and a mouse then made the best of its free gift.

That really sums up the hedgerow harvest – it is nature's free gift. It is one more reason why we should respect and protect our hedgerows. Not only does a hedgerow harvest look attractive and add colour at the change of the year. It is also providing vital food for the many creatures that share our countryside with us. Wild hedgerows ought not to be an 'amenity option', they should be a requirement.

8

What a Cow

———

I am not a happy man. Four of our BSE free cattle have just gone away for incineration. Their departure was sickening; they were all in superb condition, yet they had to be transported to an approved BSE slaughterhouse at Brentwood, killed and burnt; it is a wicked, senseless waste. What makes the situation even worse is the fact that if these cattle were simply to be set alight, why couldn't the Mafia of MAFF have put them down on the farm, with a lethal injection, instead of making them face the trauma and stress of transportation to Brentwood? The carcasses could then have been transported to the incinerator.

Of course I know the answer to my own question; MAFF will say that the cost of injections is too high, and so on economic grounds the live cattle must be transported. It is the usual answer – economics and 'efficiency' before humanity, decency and common sense.

The cost of BSE is an interesting one; according to MAFF the cost of compensating for BSE will be a modest £1 billion per year. And who will pay? As usual that is easy to answer too – you, me and every other tax payer in Europe. Those people who will not be paying are the feed manufacturers who created the crisis; the bureaucrats who allowed animal remains to be fed to herbivores and the politicians of all the major parties who nodded the various approvals through Parliament. It is another example of our wonderful MPs being totally unaccountable for their ignorant and hugely expensive actions. Let's give them another 26% pay rise for their sheer nerve.

I have some good news and bad news on the sane cow front. Our house cow Cowslip has just given birth to her latest calf. It was an unplanned event; there she was, quietly grazing and minding her own business, when who should appear next to her but Solomon the bull. So great was his passion that he walked through two barbed wire fences and an electric fence to get to her. Alas, poor Cowslip was undone. We had not intended to breed from her this year as her last two calves led to bad cases of milk fever and we nearly lost her. Consequently as she got larger and larger and calving day approached I was concerned for her – fortunately a chemical cocktail administered shortly before calving, and a pint of calcium immediately afterwards meant that she stayed on her feet this year.

Teaching the calf to drink was a nightmare. Unfortunately Cowslip's udder is so large that we can't get a bucket underneath, and so we no longer use her milk. The calf had the same problem – how to get its head below this enormous swinging structure, with a teat at each corner, without being flattened. Several times a day, for a week, both me and the calf were on all fours under the udder; me persuading the calf that the long pink thing was something to suck, while the calf was only intent on sucking my fingers and hair. Calf sucked hair could become a fashion of the future as my curls have become even curlier. Fortunately mother and calf are both doing well and the quickly growing calf, imaginatively called Cowslip 5, is doing well.

The bad news about Cowslip is that her presence on the farm has stopped us joining the Government's idiotic Beef Assurance Scheme – a scheme that sounds good, and looks good, but few people can join. MAFF has quite rightly been criticised for master-minding a scheme of mass slaughter which includes a huge majority of perfectly healthy no-risk cattle. MAFF claims, quite absurdly, that all cattle over 30 months old must be incinerated as BSE risks, even from herds and areas that have never seen BSE and will never get BSE.

The reason for all this is to kill as many cattle as possible so that the BSE illiterates of Brussels will again accept British beef. It is a numbers game; morality, honesty, or even good science is of no account. Let's kill as many animals as possible over 30 months old to make our European masters happy.

So great has been the outrage of traditional livestock farmers concerning the 30 month rule, as their animals are hardly mature at that time, that the Government has come up with its Beef Assurance Scheme; it allows BSE free beef herds to keep their animals up to 42 months. Fine – apart from the fact few people can join. It is a piece of PR confetti as the MAFFIA's real intention is to keep killing as many animals as possible to impress Europe. We cannot join because of Cowslip the single house cow. She is classified as 'milk production', although she supplied milk only for our own use; she lived in the same way as our BSE free beef animals and was fed the same food, but her presence prevents us from qualifying for the scheme – there are hundreds of farmers with a solitary house cow in exactly the same position – it is a scheme aimed at ineligibility.

The Brown brothers of Peterborough run one of the best butchers' shops in East Anglia. They produce quality Galloway beef on the Nene Washes. Part of their grazing is an SSSI – good, traditional, unimproved pasture. Surprise, surprise, they are ineligible – some of their cattle have been on their land for less than four years, although they can all be traced back to BSE free herds in Scotland. It is clear that the bureaucrats don't want farmers like the Browns joining the scheme either. The biggest insult however is the cost for joining the scheme – £35 per herd, plus £3.35 per animal. It is nothing less than a tax on good, disease free herds – incredible.

9

Bring Back the Stocks

It's a hard life being a juvenile delinquent these days, after all how do you choose your solicitor and fill in your Legal Aid form if you can't do joined up writing? It is one of my great regrets that I was born in 1943 and not 1983, or even 93. If only things had been different when I was young; I was not a hooligan, but at a very early age my mother slapped my legs simply for flicking porridge at my brother across the breakfast table. It was child abuse; for such a good shot I should have been praised and the porridge replenished – punishment was outrageous.

Then there was my father; at the age of eight, I was wrongly given out when playing cricket on the lawn. It was only right therefore that I should knock all the stumps out of the ground with the bat and throw the ball out of the garden. Instead of being seen as an act of self-expression – the 'right' of every child, my manic father caught hold of me, put me over his knee and walloped me with the spiky batting gloves. With atrocities such as these committed against me regularly during childhood and teen-hood, is it surprising that I have turned out as I have? Today I could have made a small fortune in damages, with social workers and child psychiatrists seeing to my every need and whim.

Of course I do not actually believe any of this. I am grateful to my parents for correcting me, sometimes dramatically, as I had definite hooligan tendencies and some people think I still have them. What does outrage me is the fact that in real life a child is actually allowed to take his step-father to a European Court and it is highly likely that 'Europe' will ban all corporal punishment. In my view what the child wants is a visit from my old mother for a good leg slapping, as does his solicitor. Unfortunately it is a

23

sign of the times, punishment is no longer seen as retribution to fit the crime – by an increasing number of social manipulators, punishment is seen as the crime. Correction, discipline and retribution are counter-productive and as they gradually disappear into history, crime rates, delinquency, bad manners and vandalism all soar out of control.

The punishment meted out to criminals has become a joke; 'the rule of law' is a figment of legal and political imaginations and it is the law abiding citizen who is harrassed and victimised by a growing army of bureaucrats, eurocrats, yobbos and delinquents. These days it is almost a greater crime to defend yourself on your property against criminals, than it is to break the law.

In my own village we have a spate of yobbo vandalism; bus shelters and the village pavilion have been turned into dosshouses and instead of punishment there were suggestions to give the 'young people' their own caravan on the recreation ground to 'do their own thing', i.e smoke pot, get drunk and end up in flames as the caravan ignites. Fortunately a few local reactionaries stopped it – by some they were thought to be most unfair.

Only today I heard of an unemployed thirty-year-old actually being prosecuted. For driving through a fox hunt at top speed, blowing his horn, and crashing into a horse, this poor victim of society was disqualified from driving for six months and fined £100 with £75 costs. With legal aid, six witnesses in attendance, lawyers and policemen present, this gentleman's anti-social behaviour put lives in danger and cost thousands of pounds to bring to court. It cost him six months on a bike and £175 – British justice – hoho.

Even better was a farmer who had didecoys (travellers) drive onto his farm in broad daylight and steal his horse-trailer. The next day he saw it on an official camp-site for travellers at the other end of the county. He reported it to a police force – which produces wonderful glossy brochures about combating crime – and the police refused to go and reclaim it as 'that would be far too dangerous' – yes, a 'no-go' area (one of many) in ordinary rural Britain.

I suppose if the police had gone in and made an arrest, then the travellers would have complained to the European Court of Justice, arguing that arrest was an act of racism against a minority group and that thieving was part of the travellers' traditional way of life. The only minorities that have no rights in Britain today, it would appear, are those that hunt, shoot and fish.

The reasons for the current state of lawlessness throughout the country is obvious; no discipline at home or school; the decline in religious belief; no competitive sport at school to use up energy and find out how to win and lose; no national service to hoik hooligans into a different environment; mobility of labour which leads to rootlessness and a lack of continuity, community and responsibility and a general belief that everybody can do their own thing. Then to cap it all there is no longer any fear of a deterrent. When the law finally trundles into action, it is the victim who is often made to feel more guilty than the criminal. When an individual is mugged or burgled, he or she can be traumatised and left in fear. The yobbo, if caught and found guilty, will more often than not be given a conditional discharge or community service. Community service must be one of the longest running jokes in British legal history – it usually involves long periods of loafing, sitting and smoking. What it teaches is not contrition or that the punishment fits the crime, but that it is easy to loaf and sit while smoking – courtesy of social security payments.

The answer to all this came to me the other day. I was in a Hertfordshire village looking at an ancient set of stocks. Because of their antiquity there was a notice nearby asking visitors to keep off – so in keeping with modern Britain school children were climbing all over them, while their teachers looked on smoking. The poor Hertfordshire village was suffering an urban invasion from Islington – no wonder the ever smiling Mr Blair sends his son to a school out of the area. There it was, the answer to our crime and punishment problem – stocks. They should have been in use then, not for the children climbing over them, but the teachers doing nothing to prevent the bad behaviour. The teachers should have been held for a night and a day to allow the villagers from Hertfordshire to visit Islington and behave badly there. To help the teachers meditate, those locals left in charge should have pelted them periodically with handfuls of mud and duck droppings from the nearby pond. Perhaps, very rapidly the teachers would learn the meaning of responsibility and respect.

Didecoys in the stocks would be a wonderful challenge. Their vans and caravans could be dismantled before their very eyes – the car radios removed, the good tyres taken and the light units sold to the highest bidder. Instead of being pelted with rubbish, they could be washed, scrubbed and shampooed ten times a day.

Yobbos in the stocks would be a weekend entertainment. They would be humiliated and seen by all as un-cool. They would be made to comb their hair with partings, wear suits, carry handbags and then be pelted with tomato ketchup, BSE burgers, Coca Cola and all the revolting edible substances whose litter they usually leave in their wake.

By the same token village speed limit breakers would look well in the stocks. The commuting stockbroker or solicitor made to have a Mohican haircut, wear leathers and then be pelted with the traditional substances of the farm yard. They would never speed again. Yes, that is the answer to rural crime, urban crime and national crime – bring back the stocks – it would solve crime and punishment and provide many hours of harmless, healthy fun for the locals.

10

A Gay Time

———

My ewes have been looking at me very strangely lately. I have been arriving regularly with a bucket of food, to keep them bucket-trained, while they have been waiting patiently for me to turn-up pulling the blue trailer, containing Douglas, the pedigree Suffolk tup. It's rather unfair calling him Douglas, as he seems to have a much greater understanding of life than the ex Tory minister Douglas Hoggwash.

Sadly I have been too busy to take Douglas to his harem on time; next year's lambs will be the latest ever. There have simply been too many meetings and dinners to attend and so tupping has had to wait. It is a strange reflection of modern values that I can earn more money from staggering to my feet and speaking, after an enormous pre-Christmas dinner, than I can by proper shepherding.

On one cold frosty dusk the ewes got their revenge. As soon as the Daihatsu lurched to a halt they were bleating at the gate. Then, once they had spied the bucket of food, their bleating reached a crescendo. There is a simple rule when dealing with sheep and buckets at the same time – keep your legs closed. Alas, just as I had both hands on the bucket, ready to empty it, I forgot the rule and a ewe shot between my legs as it tried to anticipate the fall of food. Unfortunately, being of a refined, delicate build, the ewe was wider than the gap between my legs; I've heard of legs so bowed that the owner could not stop 'a pig in a poke'. My legs were so narrow that I did stop this lamb in a jam, and found myself whipped off my feet riding bareback – not clutching reins, but the bucket.

It is at times like this that the whole of life rushes past – I knew what would happen, sooner or later; the momentum of the sheep, coupled with the inconvenience of the bucket would see me roll off the back of the beast. Then what? Would I sprain my ankle or break an arm? The fall came sooner than later; after twenty yards my feet shot skywards and I performed a backward roll, off the ewe and into the mud. All my limbs seemed sound but it had suddenly become exceptionally dark; even the stars had disappeared. I sat up; it was still pitch black – then it registered, the bucket was on my head, all the food had emptied over me and the sheep were in the process of eating me as well as the 'ewe pencils'. To make matters worse, from beneath me I could feel that I had landed on something warm and steaming.

I got up, shook myself down and returned to the car, suffering only from loss of dignity. Then I realised that I had lost something else – my car keys. In darkness, with the feeble rays of a new moon, every fallen leaf reflects light like a set of car keys. I gave up and walked home a mile across the fields to collect my reserve set and at the dinner, later that night, my neighbours kept insisting that they could smell sheep; I wonder where the smell came from?

Although Douglas the tup has yet to arrive, Father Christmas and his reindeer arrived exactly on time again this year. But something very strange has happened to him; I don't know if he is on drugs, steroids or what, but he seems to have grown. Last year he was fat and squat, this year he was tall and lean. Fortunately the hordes of children who arrived to see him did not notice that his name had changed from Ken to John, as even Father Christmas gets flu.

Amazingly Father Christmas visited me this year after an absence of several years. I don't know why he stopped coming and I can't think why he suddenly found out where I lived again. I am also puzzled by the size of the present he left on my bed – the 480 pages of Richard Mabey's *Flora Britannica*. If he had many copies of this weighty tome for delivery, how did his sledge manage to get airborne and how did he prevent himself from falling like a stone from the top of my chimney pot, into the firegrate? I think these are important questions. Perhaps, like heavy lorries, European directives are allowing heavier sledges to traverse the Christmas night sky these days.

Flora Britannica is a magnificent book and took Richard Mabey five years to complete. It contains serious botany, folklore and simple country wisdom all under one cover. Being so heavy it has one other great advantage – once a flower has been found and correctly identified, the tome can be used as a near perfect flower press.

My carol singing has been ruined this year by politically correct carols. What is wrong with tradition and traditional language? There I was singing heartily 'Good Christian men rejoice, with heart and soul and voice', when everybody else was singing 'Good Christians all rejoice'. Thankyou 'Baptist Praise and Worship' – how much longer will it be before we sing 'While sheep-herding persons watch their flocks by night' and 'We three wise people from the Far East are'?

We had political correctness on the CRT land the other day. We welcomed Elliot Morley, a politician with far more countryside knowledge than most of his ilk. But I held my breath, would Elliot Morley be male or female? George Eliot was a woman, so Elliot Morley could have been a man. Astonishingly, although he looked like a man, and spoke like a man, he described himself as a 'person'. He is a Labour 'spokesperson'. I know English is a living language, but all this political correctness in language is very sad.

11

The Puma Rumour

———

At last I have safely returned my neighbour's ram. He has not been worried by the beast's long holiday of course, in a winter such as this it has been one less mouth for him to feed. Fortunately there were no hiccups on the return journey – but I still have nightmares about the trip to fetch him.

Whenever towing it is a good idea to develop a routine so that the trailer, muckspreader or whatever, is totally secure. I use an old horse-trailer for my sheep and always use the same routine – except on this occasion when my nephew Andrew came to lend a helping hand. As we had not seen one another for some time we were exchanging gossip and there was an enormous amount to exchange; consequently I left him to fix the trailer's socket onto the Daihatsu's ball and he left it for me. In other words the trailer was left balancing on the car, with nothing to hold it but gravity.

We went along the local A road, down the village High Street and halfway to the next village, with the trailer held on by gravity; then we hit bumps. I glanced into a wing mirror and was horrified, I was being over-taken by my own trailer. Up the road an old lady looked startled as her mini was being approached by the trailer on her side of road; the postman could not believe his eyes.

Suddenly the trailer's brakes held, it performed a graceful 440 degree pirouette in the middle of the road before hurtling just past a lamp-post and into the ditch. The old lady screeched to a halt; the postman dropped his bike as he shook with laughter, and then various people emerged from houses or stopped their cars to see the sight. As is always the case at times of extreme embarrassment, I knew every one. They all thought it was extremely amusing. 'Well that's a nifty piece of parking', 'If you use ditches you can always find somewhere to park I suppose'.

With so many mockers at least we had volunteers to stop the trainer flipping right over when it came to be pulled out. With the Daihatsu pulling and a rope fixed to the roof of the trailer, with assorted bodies hanging on, the trailer came out of the ditch like a rabbit from a hole. Amazingly it was still in perfect order, without a scratch or a dent. Nobody had been killed; the lamp-post was still upright and we continued on our way, an hour late, with the trailer firmly fixed this time onto the tow bar.

But alas, the worst was still to come. We picked up the ram and quickly delivered him to the ewes. But something was wrong, I seemed to have more sheep than I owned – then the ugly truth dawned, all a neighbour's awful Texel rams had broken into my sweet, innocent girls and beaten the Suffolk ram by a short head. I'm dreading lambing; the thought of my beautiful sheep having their lines uglified by a Texel is almost too much to bear.

Lambing will be interesting for another reason. Will I be visited by the lamb eater of two years ago? I have changed my mind on that incident, when a six week old, healthy lamb was eaten in a single night. Originally I believed it to be foxes or a rogue badger. Now I believe that I was visited by the black 'Fen Tiger'. The quickest way to find out if the beast really exists would be to ask for a team of Ministry investigators to arrive. They went to

Bodmin to look for the 'Beast' and found nothing. With MAFF's record of investigation, their lack of evidence almost certainly confirms that the Beast of Bodmin exists.

My conversion to the escaped puma theory for Cambridge-shire has resulted from a number of strange incidents. The autumn following the loss of the lamb I was walking along the banks of the brook with assorted conservationists and EA men when we saw something black slink out of some blackthorn. I only caught a fleeting glimpse and thought 'a wet fox'. Seconds later we saw a fox – it was still dry and almost sandy coloured. A few days later a man in the next village was taking his dog for a walk in an old orchard. Suddenly a muntjac deer overtook him at speed 'With a black puma right behind'.

The following summer I went with the CRT treasurer, Ken Gifford, to look at a pile of wood – you can enjoy all sorts of delights in the country. I was puzzled, once at the wood. I was concerned that Bramble, my little lurcher, would not come within fifty yards of the pile. I turned to whistle Bramble and looked back to Ken – he had gone white and his mouth was open. 'I have just seen a large black cat slink over to those brambles – it was huge, it must have been a puma'. He looked genuinely shocked.

A fortnight ago I came across the feathered remains of three dead herons. I was puzzled; I have seen numerous herons killed by foxes – they are usually just headless. But these herons had been well and truly scoffed. A few day's later the CRT's tenant farmer took his dog into the same field. 'She went ballistic. Her hackles went up; she barked like I've never heard her before and she wouldn't leave my side'. Then he caught a fleeting glimpse of something large and black run up the side of the old railway bridge and cross the road. 'It was jet black – it must have been the puma'. There have been many claimed sightings in the last six months and I believe them.

Some people claim that the 'tiger' is a danger and should be hunted down before it kills baby. I believe that it should be left alone. It is obviously surviving well without causing much damage and its survival indicates that reintroducing the lynx, wolf and wild boar to Britain would be just as unobtrusive.

12

Global Dawning

The world is getting warmer, so they say. It is a claim that I believe, as I see my world gradually changing around me. It is a change that I do not want and do not welcome as I love my temperate world – a world of seasons, growth, blossom, fruit and the bare branches of winter. Each month brings fresh attractions – warm days, wet winds from the West, baking sun, dust, rain, heat, frost and snow.

In my heart I am still a child as I love snow. When snow arrives I look out of my window at the new white world and I welcome it. I commute from my bedroom to my study via the kitchen for a cup of hot tea. When it is a hard day and it's my turn to feed the cattle, my early morning journey will be slightly longer; I will walk a hundred yards to the farm, with Bramble behind me – he loves the snow, too.

Silence comes with the snow as it muffles sound; I would love to live in a quieter world and snow gives it to us until the thaw or the arrival of the lorries spreading salt. Each step on the newly fallen snow is a pleasure; it is soft and crunches underfoot. Bramble runs, jumps and rolls – he is childish too, at fourteen he has seen it all before and loves it still.

Then comes the rush hour. It is badly named as the commuters are worried for themselves and their highly polished cars, and for once they do not 'rush'. At the junction they sit huddled over their steering wheels, heaters on, hating every minute and yard. Outside the air is crisp, the skin tingles – it is wonderful and I love every moment and every footstep.

The footsteps in snow at dawn are a fascination, for they reveal the activities of the night. A fox has walked through the farmyard; it has sniffed at the door of the henhouses and left its calling card on a thistle. In the middle of the large field two foxes have circled, fought or played. In several places efforts have been made to dig out a mouse or a vole and snow and soil have been scattered. There is no sign of capture or escape.

Bird footprints show that pheasants have been scraping for seeds and at the end of their trail perfect wing-prints show the exact place of take-off. Two partridges explode into flight; they have been tucked down in long grass below the snow, keeping out of the wind and huddled for warmth. The brook looks like a picture book with grasses and rushes along the banks bent over and white, and the willows dazzling in sunlight. At the water's edge icicles hang downwards from the bank and fresh tracks show that something has left the water. The otters have been back over three years but I still become excited everytime I see their signs. Their world changes when the snow melts, then the small, gentle brook becomes a raging torrent and spills over to its flood plain. The water becomes muddied and brown and the otters' usual places for rest and shelter are drowned. How do otters fish in such a torrent and turmoil? And where do they rest? It is surprising and reassuring to realise just how much we do not understand about the things around us.

A snipe, feeding at the water's edge, climbs into the cold sky and there are signs of more snow to come – I regard it as a promise; others regard it as a threat. At the old road over the abandoned railway line there are phantom noises; they are the noises of childhood memory. In our lowland landscape the railway bridge was our mountain, our resort, for winter sports. As the few cars compacted the snow into ice the bridge became our Cresta Run. There were home made sledges made from wood and held together with nails and string; there were simple flat boards with no method of braking or steering, and there was our green, metal, garden stepladder. Flat on the ground with a body on top it was the fastest thing on ice; there were races, thrills, spills, laughter, tears, cuts and bruises and the next day we would be back for more. Sadly now the salt lorries prevent a new generation of home-grown winter sports and in any case the cement lorries, the buses, and the commuters would make the village Cresta Run a place of danger, not laughter. Alas, many of today's children are missing childhood and, like their parents, they are simply waiting for the thaw.

Beyond the bridge is a newly planted spinney. In the summer some people look at it with concern. The land between the young trees is not trimmed or weeded, it becomes overgrown and full of 'weeds'. In the snow there are many signs – there have been hundreds of small birds sheltering and feeding among the twisted broken stalks. The weeds have left thousands of seeds on and in the ground – larks, finches, buntings and sparrows have found a source of winter survival.

Starlings drop down into the snow to look for seeds or hidden cowpats containing grubs – life has to go on. If the snow lingers with frost, the cold can claim many casualties, but even so their death means that others survive and the foxes eat many victims of ice and hunger.

The farmyard in snow looks like a picture post card and when the heat of the sun causes a slight daytime thaw great icicles a yard or more long hang from the thatch of the farmhouse.

Of course some will say that my view of snow is entirely romantic. It is not, for I love those days too when the snow falls all day and the wind turns it into a storm. Where the wind lifts it off the fields and funnels it through holes in the hedges creating blizzards, great drifts form. Snow turns to ice on hats and boots and the cold signals the time to grow my winter beard. Once out of the cold the other great joy of snow sets in – thawing out in front of a log fire with a glass of sloe gin in my hand. With a winter like this who wants global warming?

13

Wise Foxes

A book I cannot recommend too highly is *The Covenant of the Wild* by Stephen Budiansky. It begins – 'For two million years we were hunters; for ten thousand years we were farmers; for the last one hundred years we have been trying to deny it all'. It is a mini-masterpiece; what he describes and explains is how the suburban view of nature has come to dominate – how people separated from nature view wildlife and landscapes through rose-tinted spectacles – it is the 'cuddly bunny' syndrome re-visited.

I was reminded of this great separation from nature several weeks ago when I had the misfortune to talk to a member of The League Against Cruel Sports – I suppose he was called Kevin, or Darren, most of them seem to be, and I apologise to any shooting or hunting Kevin's or Darren's, I am afraid you are outnumbered. The innocent Kevin came out with a most astonishing statement, which was also his main plank against hunting, and, if I understood him correctly, against any sort of fox control, that 'the fox in Britain has no natural predators'.

I was flabbergasted. I have long expressed the view that most of the objections to hunting are unsoundly based – read Labour's amusing Elliot Morley on the subject – but this was a case of basic wildlife illiteracy. Even forgetting the cubs that are taken by golden eagles, Man (sorry Elliot Morley – Person) has been the fox's biggest and most natural predator for at least 2,010,100 years. Do the fox-lovers believe that Man is not a part of nature?

For two million years the fox was undoubtedly hunted; it competed with those early hunter/gatherers and so they would have got rid of the competition at every opportunity. In addition, those hunter/gatherers in cold and temperate climates would have killed foxes for their fur. Fox fur is warm and comfortable and it is one of my ambitions to get a fox fur Davy Crockett hat and wear it every time I go to London in the winter. Unfortunately I will have a long wait as nobody seems to cure skins anymore.

For ten thousand years, man the farmer/hunter/gatherer has also chased off foxes. With the domestication of hens, sheep, goats and even pigs, the competition between man and foxes became even greater. I disagree with Stephen Budiansky slightly; I believe 'the great denial' has come in the last forty years, not one hundred years. In my childhood, ordinary village people were still the natural predators of the fox. It seems incredible to me now, as I see several foxes each week, that I did not see my first wild, red fox until I was well into my teens – there were simply hardly any foxes about. In fact it is true to say that because of the persecution of the fox at that time, without hunting and the preservation of foxes for sport, they would have become extinct.

The reason for the persecution of foxes around my village was simple. In those days virtually every house in the High Street, and every farm, had free range hens. Consequently any fox that did appear, rapidly disappeared; snares went up in virtually every hole in every hedge and if Reynard avoided them, he was shot. It was for the same reason that during my childhood I rarely saw a magpie; the stealers of chicks and eggs simply were not tolerated.

The other great pressure on foxes came from rabbit-trappers. Before myxomatosis there were men who made a living, or part of a living from rabbit-trapping, using both snares and gin traps. If a snare line was visited by a fox, then a gin would be set and the fox removed. With the arrival of disease and the abolition of gin traps an enormous pressure was taken off the fox. Then of course the living and shopping habits of ordinary people changed; it became too much trouble to keep hens in the back garden – eggs were purchased from the village shop and then the supermarket and the average fox had absolutely nothing to worry about. The fox's main predator, stopped predating.

So, rather than the fox having 'no natural predator', the fox found itself in the position of having a natural predator that decided not to predate. Our friendly Kevin from the League should think about this and consider what has happened since the fox has had no competition. The facts are that the fox population has rocketed and I believe that it is higher than ever before. Only a few gamekeepers, poultry farmers and huntsmen control its numbers, and over most of Britain it lives and multiplies happily and safely.

When I mentioned all this to our fox lover (I love foxes too, in moderation, not saturation), he mentioned another well worn phrase – the 'natural balance'. He, bless him, thought the fox population would find its 'natural balance'. Again poor Kevin showed the width of the great sub-urban divide. There can be no 'natural balance' when virtually the whole of Britain's landscape is un-natural. Our un-natural, man-made landscape has helped the fox and enabled it to become totally out of balance. In a natural world, the fox population would be controlled entirely by the natural food available. In winter especially, a high percentage of foxes would die through lack of food. Today, the reverse is true, large numbers of foxes are surviving the winter because of the food we make available to them.

During the 'hard' months of winter the fox now lives quite easily. There is a great variety of food available, from bird tables, cattle troughs and road kills – the amount of fresh meat at the roadside for foxes, crows and magpies is quite remarkable. The other great favourite is worms and whenever cultivation takes place during the winter I notice the fox droppings turn to the colour of the soil as they switch to eating worms. This too is comparatively new; with large, powerful machines more winter cultivation is possible and the food supply covers many acres. Certainly a fox can glean worms from a cultivated field when it would find few worms available in grass. As a result large numbers of foxes are living through the winter, in good condition, ready for the spring. During the spring and summer the artificial food sources are still available, so are the natural ones, the ground nesting birds – grey partridges, lapwings and even skylarks. If the birds themselves are not taken, then the young and eggs certainly are and there is little doubt that predation by foxes is a contributory factor in the decline of a number of species.

This year along the Norfolk and Suffolk coastline there has been a great plague of foxes and they have caused much havoc, this time with tern colonies, redshank and avocets. Because of this new predators are arriving on the scene; now most conservation bodies are culling foxes – some not very successfully. Their task is not helped by the animal rights activists who are actually live-trapping foxes in towns and releasing them in the country. Surely this should be made illegal? It is unfair on the foxes – most of whom are soon killed anyway, and unfair on the wildlife where they are released.

So thank you Kevin for reminding me about foxes. The message is that Man has always competed with foxes and perhaps we should start competing even harder. If we don't, we can say good-bye to the grey partridge, the lapwing, and the avocet, and frankly, I prefer them to suburbanites called Kevin.

14

Bad Dogs, Good Dogs and Mad People

This Chapter is almost a continuation of the last. I have had several letters recently all upbraiding me for having genuinely held views in support of hunting, based on conservation, tradition and individual freedom. The common words in these letters have been predictable, 'killers', 'barbarians', 'bloodthirsty' etc. This is interesting, for without a doubt the biggest killers of wildlife in Britain today are cars and lorries – yet where are the protests? Where are the 'car saboteurs', and on a more practical level, where are the 'wildlife speed limits' to try to save our badgers, otters, foxes and barn owls from needless death and injury?

Only the other day I found a fox about forty yards from a minor road. Its back legs were broken and it had dragged itself into a clump of brambles to die. Two summers ago, a length of road close to here was littered with dead birds and animals – two foxes, two badgers, a muntjac deer and a whole brood of pheasant chicks – a friend described it as like driving through a 'dead zoo'. But nothing is done and presumably if lower speed limits were put on country roads to stop the slaughter, the roads lobby would complain about the economic damage being done to the road haulage industry. So we tolerate this daily carnage; 'ban hunting' – nice and easy isn't it?

Sadly, it is not just wild animals that are killed in thousands – family pets go the same way. Most killed by cars going too fast, driven by drivers quite unconcerned that they are speeding through peoples' homes and lives.

I nearly lost Bramble the other day. I could not believe it. He has been my constant companion for fourteen years, and apart from slight deafness he is fine. He is seldom on a lead. He is a farm dog; he is constantly on and off the tractor, hunting for mice and eating disgusting objects – it is all part of the privilege of being a farm dog. When I am stuck at the typewriter, he will sometimes wander up to the farm on his own – he knows the way; he is under control; he is not lost – he lives here. Fortunately only two old ladies tried to pick him up and take him to the local dog's home during the summer.

The other evening at dusk he was out of control. A ginger rabbit sprinted out of the farmhouse garden, over the road and made for a nearby spinney. Bramble set off after it in spirited geriatric pursuit. The light was poor and drizzle had started. I whistled him and he did not come. I whistled again and he came out of the darkness at the trot, just as a large black car, roared around the corner, breaking the speed limit by at least 20 mph. I was mortified; everything seemed to occur in slow motion as the inevitable happened. The car accelerated through Bramble; there was a loud bang and my beloved dog cartwheeled down the road and lay in a heap by the verge – the car driver did not lift his foot from the accelerator for a second and disappeared into the dusk. I was sure Bramble was dead; I could feel grief and despair welling up – then he moved. He stood up, shook himself, looked around and came to me. His nose was bleeding, but nothing else seemed wrong; no bones were broken – I carried him home as a precaution – he had been a lucky dog – simply doing things that country dogs do. We are both just unlucky to have many non-country people living among us who do not understand the lifestyles and values around them. (For eight years I have had high-frequency whistles on my car, and have hit no bird or animal since. They can be obtained from the British Hedgehog Preservation Society).

Hippy is another lucky dog. He is a Jack Russell terrier and lives four miles away, as the crow flies. One morning his owner got up and found a puddle by the kitchen door. Hippy looked sheepishly at her, she looked angrily at him; Hippy was thrown out. The next morning it happened again; this time Hippy was scolded and unceremoniously booted out. It got worse, and each morning his aerial trajectory out of the door grew higher. Out of desperation his owner took him to the vet. 'Yes', she said, 'Hippy must have an infection' and she plunged a thermometer up one of his orifices – he growled and snarled, he was not amused; after a regular scolding, now it was humiliation.

Even after a course of anti-biotics, the dreaded puddle was still on the carpet every morning and Hippy's aerial adventures grew and grew. The vet's next piece of wisdom was: 'Collect a sample of water from the puddle and we will get it analysed'. Sure enough in the morning the puddle was there and Hippy was booted out in disgrace. 'Funny', his angry owner thought as she gazed into the liquid, 'there's cabbage in it'. She looked again – oh no, it had not been Hippy leaking after all, but the dishwasher. All that shouting, booting out, and of course, the thermometer being plunged up his bottom, all for a leaking dishwasher. He was given Bonios, tins of Chum, and even allowed to sit on the settee. Now, whenever the dishwasher is switched on he leaps under his beanbag snarling.

Sadly poor Hippy's traumas were not over. He was taken to a farm just north of Cambridge for a few days. Within hours he had vanished. No dogs' homes knew of him; the police could not find him; he had disappeared into thin air. Five days later a phone call to a dogs' home revealed a chance conversation saying that a chunky Jack Russell had been found in Sainsbury's car park in Thetford. It was Hippy; two days later and he would have been given away. But how did he get there? No doubt somebody saw a 'dear little dog', put it in their car and let it out miles from its home. We British are a nation of animal-lovers, you know!

15

Pin-striped Peasants

———

I now have a pair of binoculars up in my roof. The roof is where I put my thoughts onto an ancient, obsolete Amstrad. It is the perch too from where I can view my garden's birds, and this winter it is bursting with them. But now, apparently I must use my binoculars to search for other, newer incomers to the countryside – 'downshifters'. Yes, the countryside is gradually being invaded by a new breed of immigrant. Once it was the upwardly mobile buying up all our village houses. Now, so it is said, some of the buyers are deliberately trying to become downwardly mobile – they are 'downshifters'. These poor souls are apparently tired of a society based as it is on cash-flow capitalism and rampant consumerism. After years of stashing away capital and consuming slightly more than everybody else, they suddenly want to lead simpler, more fulfilling lives, they want the time 'to enjoy the good things of life'.

At first when I heard all this I assumed that it meant a return to the 'good-life syndrome' and my binoculars were looking for middle-aged hippies with baggy jumpers, jeans, and ancient, original duffle coats, trying to milk a goat, bake home made bread – yes, in an Aga – and growing vegetables where most people had flowering borders, rockeries and weed-free lawns. But no, these dwindling 'good lifers' are not the 'downshifters'. Downshifters are, apparently, an entirely new phenomenon – they don't uproot from London or Manchester and re-root in a remote Scottish glen or East Anglian village for isolation and simplicity – they uproot and 'downshift' to a rural area, but they take all their sophisticated Twentieth Century toys, comforts and technology with them. It is not a duffle coat living, or even Barbour – it is Goretex.

The 'downshift' is in effect a 'horizontal shift', for although the 'downshifters' move locations, they take sophistication with them, not daring to adopt total simplicity or rusticity.

Spotting a downshifter is easy. A removals van arrives at the old cottage. The next week a central heating firm arrives; a BMW is in the garage and the residents are never seen. The only way to attempt to view them is to deliver the church magazine. Through the window you can see a fax machine, a washing up machine and the Aga has been taken out for a completely new all electric kitchen. The couple inside are wet; at four o'clock in the afternoon they have just had a shower. The postman says they are wet first thing in the morning too; what are they doing tucked away down there requiring two showers a day?

Then the garden takes shape – herbs, roses and mange tout, yes, mange tout – flat peas with no taste that make even the maggots flat. Then the penny drops, there are 'downshifters' in the village already; the date of their arrival can be traced back to the first plate of mange tout in the vegetable classes at the annual village Flower Show, five years ago. Mange tout, aubergines and courgettes, the staple summer diet of downshifters, and maintained throughout the winter courtesy of the lovely, sustainable Mr Tesco.

I still remember with horror the first time I ate two whole

mange tout, together with three slices of almost raw carrot and a sliver of tasteless courgette. It was in a top London restaurant where I was being treated to 'lunch', with Gordon Beningfield. At the end of the meal, still famished, we thanked our host and bought some fish and chips.

So sadly, downshifting is really a fad, based on myth. The downshifters are in effect early retirement dropouts and their country hideaways rapidly become suburban and urban capsules – remote boxes full of all the luxury consumer aids for comfortable living from their earlier lives.

To enjoy their opportunities to the full the downshifters should study the lives of those of us who have been shifting downwards for years. They really should choose simple country living instead of simply transferring their suburban ways into the country.

My life is so simple that it can be followed very easily. The first thing to learn about the country is that it has seasons and the temperature falls in winter. As it gets colder you do not simply turn the heater up – you put on more clothes. I was staggered recently in the local pub when assorted people were complaining about the cold; I was steaming. Then it was revealed, I was the only person wearing longjohns. How can anybody get through a country winter in comfort without longjohns? When I have visitors to my house, most come, take their coats off and sit down. Five minutes later they stand up, get their coats, re-dress and sit down fully clad, while I'm still sweltering.

Food is not a problem; mange tout is out, together with French golden digusting apples. People moving into the country should eat real, seasonal country food. At the moment it might be meat pudding and swede; dumplings and parsnips, stuffed marrow or pheasant and brussels – who wants Argentinian runner beans and new potatoes when real food can still be had straight from the garden?

Then come the rural mod cons; I haven't got a CD player, washing machine, washing up machine, shower or central heating. I have a sink, a bath and a coal shed and I have absolutely no desire to have what I haven't got. I bath on the longest day and the shortest day and life is simple, comfortable and enjoyable. I think I should start courses in real rural down-shifting. I must stop now – the mobile phone is ringing.

16

Wild Life; Wild Water

———

Africa has fascinated me for years; its wildlife, its history, its heat and yes, even its violence. Africa is violent and always has been violent; it is a harsh place where the need to survive seems to dominate, from the smallest shrew, to the mighty elephant and encompassing everything in between including man.

It has drawn Europeans for generations. The stories of those early pioneers Livingstone, Speke, Burton and Selous are full of hardship, danger, achievement and adventure. Adventure is important; today history is being rewritten. You read of the European advance in Africa; the politically correct version is all about greed, commerce, exploitation, racial domination, etc. In other words, the modern version of the white man in Africa is sheer bunkum. Some people who went to Africa were greedy and scheming, but most were adventurers; Men (and a few women) who wanted the challenge of new places, dangerous wild animals and the presence of a few 'savages' thrown in for good measure. Unfortunately those early settlers had no time to be anthropologists as Zulu spears went winging towards them and so the Zulu culture was lost to them – the Zulus were seen as 'savages'.

The man who epitomises the spirit of those early Europeans was Frederick Courtney Selous, adventurer, explorer, big-game hunter and naturalist. He was a man who travelled vast distances, writing about his experiences and meeting dangers

44

almost every day. He was a remarkable man, killed in action in the old Tanganyika during the First World War at the age of 64. His writings on his wanderings and hunting still make fascinating reading. A couple of years ago I was privileged to interview Raoul Millais, the artist; at over ninety years old he is a man of great wit and wisdom. I was fascinated; one of his godfathers was Frederick Courtney Selous. He described this wonderful, alert, outstanding man; talking to him about his early memories made history live and Selous sounded like a man with an astonishing presence.

I write all this because in the long and tedious BBC television series on Cecil Rhodes, at vast expense, Selous is made to appear as dull and boring as everybody else. Rhodes is painted as a grasping neohomosexual and the whole wasted opportunity seems to be an exercise in political correctness. If only I had been given millions of pounds to make a series about the pioneer days of Africa. The fact that white Africa was, and still is largely a male culture seems to have totally escaped the author – the fact that Rhodes surrounded himself with men is somehow given a deeply sexual significance; sadly that may be the case in Television Centre, but even today that is not the case in the African bush.

I have been to the country initially named after Cecil Rhodes many times. I saw Rhodesia in war, when at times it appeared that a white skin and turned me into 'big game', or at least 'fat game', and I have seen the new Zimbabwe at peace. It is ironic, at war, the aim was to throw out the whites; at peace Europeans are desperately wanted, as tourism provides much needed revenue to help Zimbabwe survive and prosper.

I hope that people will visit the country. I want Zimbabwe to prosper, and if tourism is one of the ways to help it, then forget Skegness and Bognor, try Victoria Falls and Kariba. Visiting Africa has two great bonuses. The first is that any visitor to Zimbabwe who leaves his Harare Hotel and goes into the bush will realise the great achievement of those early pioneers. The shallowness of politically correct judgements and television series will quickly be seen.

45

The second great attraction is that it is still possible to have tremendous African adventures, with strong elements of danger; and while the adrenalin surges it is reassuring to know that some of the money being spent, whether big-game hunting, bird-watching or trying to drown in the Zambezi, is providing jobs, boosting the economy and giving money to ordinary rural communities in the bush. It is sad that some people in the safety of Britain still campaign against hunting and the proper, controlled sale of ivory, yet one hunter and two tusks can provide far more revenue to the rural people of Zimbabwe than bus loads of snap happy tourists taking photographs of sleeping lions.

On my most recent trip to Zimbabwe, a fortnight ago, I joined a party of hunters, after they had done their hunting, and even without a gun I had enough laughter and adrenalin to last me the rest of the year. I joined them after they had hunted simply because hunting is not for me; I realise that in a country where culling surplus animals is a necessity, my attitude is something of an evasion, but there it is; I don't like killing things and some people do – I am happy with that.

My first adrenalin spurt came on the famous Victoria Falls bridge – bungee jumping – I wasn't doing it. My adrenalin level went up just watching. I could not believe it; rational, normal people – in appearance anyway – jumping off a bridge over nine hundred feet above the Zambezi and saved only by a length of elastic. I thought we were supposed to be an intelligent species? The first girl I saw do it was only about eighteen, she dived with all the confidence of somebody diving head first into a swimming pool. Cold shivers went up and down my spine. Worse still I am slowly talking myself into the same thing next year; a sponsored bungee-jump for the Countryside Restoration Trust off the same bridge. I'm getting frightened just thinking about it; I hope my doctor tells me I'm too old.

The next adrenalin spurt came shortly afterwards – while flying to Mutemwa camp on the Zambezi, in Zambia; the pilot got lost. He was only looking for a huge airfield in the Caprivi Strip, once used by South Africa's security forces; all we could see were thornbushes and elephants. A quick half hour hop became a ninety minute nightmare; would we land, emergency land or crash before one of my green companions reached for the brown paper bag, that was the question. I will not reveal that the green man was none other than the great Tony Jackson – that will spoil his image. The pilot, who looked and behaved remarkably like a smiling garden gnome, finally found his position by plunging from 4000' to 40' to read a road sign – yes, that's right. .. Unfortunately as we dived, my stomach continued in a straight line and the whole thing became a race between me and Bwana Jackson, to see which one would need the brown paper bag first.

Then there were brushes with hippos; action with tiger fish and a sighting of one of the world's rarest birds – Schalow's Lourie. Another burst of adrenalin came when canoeing and a hippo appeared far too close for comfort. I was at the back steering and with great skill the 'front seat' driver managed to divert us onto a log – we were stuck fast – stand up that man responsible –.Tony Jackson again. Finally, white water rafting; what a day, what adrenalin, what fear – I swallowed half the water in the Zambezi and loved every minute of it – once it was over.

I can't wait to get back to the real Africa – it is so much better than the televised version.

17

A Party and a Parting

Christmas is a time for families and parties, but this year I had the good fortune to go to a party before Christmas that I shall never forget. It was the Ninetieth birthday party of Sir Laurens van der Post, held two days before his birthday, and four days before his death. It was a happy occasion with a house full of his family and friends – his extended family – built up through an incredible life. After recent speaking engagements in both America and Zurich he was looking tired but happy.

He took me by the arm as soon as I went to speak to him – he wanted to know about the Countryside Restoration Trust, the farm, the fields, the birds and had we had rain? As the Trust's first Patron his interest was not simply one of duty, but one of conviction and involvement. Although tired, his blue eyes were still alert and smiling. For years I had enjoyed a strange three way conversation with him, and Christopher Booker, with only two of us being present at any one time. At his party all three of us were in the same place for the first time and he enjoyed the occasion. We were then joined by the remarkable John Aspinall

There were many of his friends present, from the war, from Africa, conservation and people who had simply become friends through his personal interest and warmth. Tributes were paid to him and each time he responded – to one he even said that it had given him an idea for a new book.

The most moving tribute was from Billy Griffiths, President of St Dunstan's. He had been a prisoner of war with Laurens in a Japanese camp. There he had been forced to crawl on the ground searching for mines – he had found one, and in the resulting explosion had lost both eyes and both arms. But as he spoke of his experiences and the leadership of Laurens in the camp there was no bitterness; he spoke with pride and forgiveness and throughout his talk he smiled almost in gratitude.

It seems that everybody who knew Laurens smiled. But when did I first know him? I suppose it was as a teenager when I saw his television image on 'The Lost World of the Kalahari'. Even at that time he made me aware that my world in the English countryside was also being lost.

It was not until 1980 that I met him face to face; a personal love of Africa, conservation and his writing led me to interview him for *The Daily Telegraph*, and for a book. It was fascinating to listen to him, a man who with astonishing fluency put into words exactly how I thought and felt about the fate of our world.

He lamented the advance of the 'city mind' and how those with little understanding of the natural order of things were supervising the gradual destruction of planet. His knowledge through learning and experience were extraordinary, but his friendship and appreciation were nevertheless simple and straightforward.

I saw him many times after that; at Aldeburgh, along the sea wall where he pointed to water meadows that had been drained and fields blowing with dust; 'I never thought I would live to see dust blows in England'.

His friendship was not demanding or patronising and when he called me an 'English Bushman' I regarded it as a compliment. When he learnt one day that I was on the Balmoral estate writing 'The Wildlife of the Royal Estates', he tracked me down so that I could take coffee with him and Prince Charles. He loved the old Caledonian pine forest, the oldest of our ancient woods, and as he spoke about the area it struck me how I, one of the last English peasants, was receiving just the same friendship as an English prince.

He was always so calm and collected that when I heard him swear for the first time I was shocked. Normally in a political conversation he made it clear that he admired Margaret Thatcher, and was convinced that he was helping to turn her 'green'. Then came her notorious speech in praise of the 'car economy'. 'I don't know what's got into the bloody woman', he said with irritation.

When I asked him to become a Trustee of the Countryside Restoration Trust his response was positive and instant, as it was when he agreed to become our first Patron. In 1994 he visited the Trust land to 'open' a gate on our first field. He was moved by what we had achieved in such a short time and believed that our aims represented the 'conservation of the future'. A year later he returned, and without notes he spoke to a packed village church for the CRT's first Countryside Sunday. He held all those present, and the overflow sitting in the churchyard, enthralled. It is the first time I have ever seen a standing ovation in church.

Virtually all those who met him were touched by his generosity of spirit and already the CRT has had letters and messages from people who feel that they have lost a friend; one letter sums up the feelings well:

'I just felt the need, for who else can I tell, to say that I feel very grateful to the CRT for the wonderful experience of the First Countryside Sunday. So many times when I have been quiet, I have played the cassette. I feel very privileged to have seen and heard Sir Laurens – one of the treasured moments of my life. My favourite parts of his talk were his description of the game reserve, after the rain, and the slight chuckle in his voice that said we must be careful – the butterflies may return in such number to your land that they make a 'hullabaloo'. Whenever I hear his name I remember a sunlit day, people travelling so far to be together, and the swifts screaming overhead while we sat in your ancient church awaiting his arrival. It was wonderful'.

As I left his party Laurens caught my arm again. 'In the new year I will come and speak for you'. Before deciding to stand at the election for the Referendum Party I had discussed the pros and cons with Laurens – what a meeting it would have been with Laurens, Sir James Goldsmith and Christopher Booker on the same platform. Alas, it is now something that we shall never see.

It has been a privilege to know Laurens van der Post. The country has lost a great man; the CRT has lost its much loved Patron and I have lost a valued friend.

18

Gun Law – Car Law

All my life I have been surrounded by dangerous things; knives, pitchforks, axes, guns, bulls, boars and large farm machinery. It goes almost without saying that I have never been hurt or threatened by any of these things, because when handled properly and responsibly they pose no threat. All my main physical injuries have come from footballs, cricket balls, and yes, I have been tossed once, by a cow!

Consequently I have found all the recent hysteria about guns, exactly that – hysteria, and mostly ill-informed hysteria. It is yet another reflection of the appalling standard of our current MPs that they should have responded to it – for short-term political gain.

The gun debate has made me very angry; it arrived at a time when I was on the verge of applying for a hand-gun. I wanted a .22 pistol to help dispense lead aspirins to cage-trapped mink. We are trying to rid our local brook of mink for the benefit of kingfishers, moorhens and water voles. It seems more sensible to encourage our indigenous wildlife than the alien, North American mink. I will not now be able to have a pistol, as the vast majority of the population, and Parliament, who know nothing about them, have deemed them dangerous.

My anger over gun ignorance is made worse by the fact that in Britain today we do have rampant, ignorant killers loose in all parts of the country, and little seems to be done to control them. The mayhem does not involve guns, but cars; ten people will be killed on our roads today, as well as scores of birds and animals. Yet on Monday there will be no petitions of anger; there will be no media outrage and our politicians will be totally silent on the subject. There will be anger and sorrow, among the friends and relations of ten ordinary people, quite impotent to get some action.

If I sound angry, it is because I am angry, very angry. Recently a good local man was hit by a car and killed within a mile of the farm. For years, every weekday morning and evening he would cycle to and from Cambridge to work, along the speed-track known as the A603. He was always meticulous about the condition of his bike, his lights and his reflective clothing. He always cycled steadily and sensibly, in good weather and bad. He was hit from behind in the evening by a car, driven by a twenty-one year old; he was killed instantly.

Years ago, before many people wanted to read anything I wrote, I supplemented my meagre earnings by delivering letters. I was the village's part-time postman. I would often stop to talk to this smiling friendly cyclist – he was Tom Ap Rees, Professor in Plant Sciences at Cambridge University. Some mornings he would be rootling about in the bottom of a hedgerow; he was researching how Cuckoo-pint generated its own heat to attract insects. He loved talking about his plants, and unlike some university dons, he liked talking to ordinary people about his subject, and they enjoyed listening – I did. As he cycled home he often stopped for a solitary pint of beer, and again he found it easy to talk to the locals. His daily journey was a succession of smiles, waves and 'hallos'. The local view is simple – he was a good man, a friendly man and he was killed quite needlessly, just like numerous others each week throughout Britain.

The case of Tom Ap Rees is made even sadder by the fact that many people have, over the years, pleaded with the Police and Cambridgeshire County Council for speed checks, speed limits and traffic calming where Tom was killed, but all the requests, fears and anxieties have been ignored. As the local District Councillor I have also pestered both organisations to no avail. The County Council seems to put bureaucracy before safety, and of course they claim to be directed by 'accident injury rates'. Poor Tom Ap Rees has now become one of their statistics; prevention is evidently not better than cure – although calamity and family grief occasionally lead to reluctant action. Who will protect us from these bureacrats? And who can bring back one of the most respected academics at Cambridge?

Two years ago I wanted to drive my sheep just 100 yards along that same A603. The police said I must not do it as nearly all the traffic was speeding; it was therefore considered to be too dangerous. When I asked them to try radar traps, they said: 'the usual speed is so high it would be dangerous to wave drivers down'. This is the Police Force, the Cambridgeshire Constabulary, whose Chief Constable was actually stopped for speeding earlier in the year. In keeping with the fine example set by our MPs, he did not resign. It should also be remembered that just outside Cambridgeshire a few years ago a Labour MP was stopped at over 90mph. Neil Kinnock's reward was to be made Transport Commissioner for the mad EU.

Recently, after yet another accident on the A603, the police set up a road block to divert traffic. Those officers manning it feared for their lives as unsuspecting cars hurtled towards them. Of course, as I have written before, the answer is simple – for each parish to own and operate its own radar gun with properly trained volunteers. I would volunteer tomorrow, given the opportunity – but somehow car drivers seem to be considered above the law and many of our roads are, in effect, police 'no go' areas.

The death of Tom Ap Rees has deeply affected several village communities. We are not bothered about guns, we are however, worried, by lunatic car drivers who threaten us and our friends and relatives every single day of the year.

19

The Brain Drain

It is another spectacular flowering spring. The plum and green-gage blossom is not in the profusion of last year, which means of course that there will be fewer English plums for the supermarkets to refuse to buy, but even so there is still much bloom and the bumble bees are busy spreading pollen; I hope it means plenty of plum treacle later in the year. This year is a violet year; I can never remember seeing so many violets in gardens and on sunny banks. There are carpets of them, white, purple and mauve, where in other years they have just been in ones and twos. I have no idea why this should be, but obviously every variation in the season, or combination or seasons, brings something new. Evidently a dry autumn, a cold winter and a dry spring means abundant violets.

My pair of blackcaps are back too and gradually the dawn chorus is gaining momentum. It is not complete by a long way and is still awaiting the arrival of the whitethroats, willow warblers, swallows and swifts, but it is building up beautifully. I worry about the swallows and house martins, as the ground is already dry and solid; I hope people remember to create muddy puddles for them – life is already hard enough without the problem of how to make a nest.

Down by the brook the marsh marigolds look a picture. Those we introduced two years ago are gradually spreading and slowly they are helping the brook back to normality. Quite how or why the 'dredge-drain' water engineers of the last twenty-five years have considered it so necessary to treat marsh marigolds as a major drainage threat in our waterways is a mystery. The whole river 'drainage' industry seems nothing less than a job creation programme. I am sure that if 95% of all drainage engineers were made redundant tomorrow, nobody would notice their disappearance.

Frighteningly, the flow of the brook is already down to its late summer level, again thanks to the water engineers of the Seventies. Their drag-lines have left nothing to hold the water back during dry weather. The water we want now, flowed into the North Sea months ago courtesy of the Environment Agency in one of its former manifestations. The pond where the tadpoles are busy eating and being eaten is already down to its mid-summer level and as I write there is no sign of rain in a cloudless sky.

Last year our rainfall was only a fraction of what we wanted and already this year we are inches down; it reminds me of 1976. The difference of course between now and 1976 is that water has been privatised. Consequently in 1976, if memory serves me correctly, there were early warnings about water shortages and there were requests to put bricks into cisterns and 'share a bath with a friend', in an attempt to reduce demand. Now, with private water companies in existence the emphasis seems to be on profits, dividends and the sale of jacuzzis, rather than on the responsible use of water.

It seems to me that in East Anglia drought warnings should have been widespread as long ago as last September – but I have heard and seen nothing telling me officially of the seriousness of the situation. Of course I have heard other things – of water courses drying up and trees dying, almost certainly because of water extraction – customer service (i.e dividends) seems to take precedence over environmental responsibility.

No doubt Anglian Water will respond by saying that it is environmentally aware, indeed it does give a 'Caring for the Environment Award' every year, and in the past the Countryside Restoration Trust has won it. I wish Anglian Water would enter its own competition – I believe it would come almost last.

The astonishing thing about East Anglia's lack of water is that it is now set to be the fastest growing region in the country, and of East Anglia, Cambridgeshire is going to be the booming bubble in the booming area. In other words 60,000 new houses are planned in my District, each with taps, toilets, garden hoses, dish washers, baths, etc. etc. and already there is not the water to service them responsibly. Quite simply the planned development is not sustainable. During the industrial revolution much mindless development took place through ignorance; now in the technological age we are making the same mistakes knowingly, wantonly and cynically. Landowners and developers want the money; planners and consultants want both the money and the prestige and local councils want the increased council and business taxes so that they can spend even more.

I have been on my local district council for far too long. For most of those years I refused to go on the planning committee; I had the novel notion that as a landowner, and somebody who could profit from the planning system, I should keep off the planning committee. A view not shared by an assortment of farmers, builders, architects etc. Out of frustration with the system I am now on that committee and find that the availability of water plays no part in the planning process. The environmental consequences of over abstraction could be disastrous – but that is not a matter for planning committees – it is a Third World attitude in a First World country and is inexcusable.

The local Tories have put out a document entitled 'Rural In Touch' – 'South Cambs Villages Under Threat'. What it cynically omits to say of course is that the whole development process, of which it is warning, was set in motion by a Tory government – perhaps the document should be renamed 'Rural Out of Touch' – as usual.

20

Romantic Interlude

———

This is a good time of year, when the sap begins to rise and the traditions of the season can be enjoyed. The frogs started spawning, twenty days earlier than last year, but even so the mass *erotica aquatica* still coincided with the arrival of 'Badger' for hedge-laying. This year his arrival was part of the DT's and CRT's 'Save Our Hedges' campaign and a photographer duly arrived to capture the great Badger at work for a future occasion. The lovely lady photographer was told she would be photographing 'Badger hedge-laying'. Unfortunately she misheard her orders and understood them to be a request to photograph 'a badger egg-laying'. She was quite looking forward to this unique event; would the badger-eggs be black and white striped and did the badger lay them in a nest or bury them in a hole? Fortunately it was not April the first and she was soon pointed in the direction of 'Badger' Walker, the hedge-layer himself. Having a DT photographer present had one major disadvantage – it meant that we had to do a proper day's work instead of being diverted to other attractions.

At the same time we had a Bomford flail mower on the farm to demonstrate how good, mechanical hedge cutting can take place, at the right time of the year – after the berries have been eaten and before the birds start nesting. The demonstrator did an excellent job and was accompanied by a Bomford's representative with the unfortunate hedge cutting name of Mr Ripper.

Of course the other great traditional season activity this year has been the annual March food scare. This March it was the incredible claim that our abattoirs are in such a state that the dreaded E coli 0157 bacteria is rampant. Once again all the emphasis was wrongly directed, claiming that slaughterhouses needed to be cleaner and inspections stricter, etc. The simple facts are that the E coli outbreaks have been helped on their way by EU regulations gleefully and enthusiastically put into practice by the great and good Mr Gummer. All this took place two or three years ago, when his main job as Secretary of State for Agriculture seemed to be to close down as many small, traditional slaughter-houses as possible.

As a result of the over-stringent application of EU regulations over 400 slaughterhouses were closed down. Many of them were small, local operations which allowed animals to be killed quickly and humanely with a minimum of stress. Now we have just a few large industrialised abattoirs that are little more than killing factories, with the animals being regarded as 'units' to be turned into 'products'. Because of the numbers of animals passing through, it appears that they are more prone to diar-rhoea, which spreads the E coli, caused by the crowding, waiting and the consequent stress. So the whole theory that 'big means better' has fallen on its face, and given us a problem. Thankyou Brussels and the MAFFIA bureaucrats yet again. The answer is simple – go back to small local slaughterhouses which treat live-stock as animals, keep stress to a minimum and kill humanely.

At this time of year too I always try to go to the National Shire Horse Show at Peterborough. As I drove in last weekend I passed a flock of sheep with thick healthy fleeces. My brain then sent me a very strange message – 'why aren't those sheep sheared?' I was confused; why hadn't they been sheared? Gradually my tired mental computer sorted out the problem; last week I had been in the Falklands, the Southern Hemisphere, where shearing was late and they were still working hard to get finished; this week I am in the Northern hemisphere where shearing hasn't started.

Visiting the Falklands was wonderful; wide open spaces, pleasant people, brilliant wildlife and startlingly clean air, water and light. The birds were tremendous, and almost tame; the incredible Falklands flightless steamer duck, the famous Upland goose and the astonishing meadowlark. Farmlife was almost suicidal, it was the first time I had tried to round-up sheep by scramblebike, in fact it was the first time I had ever ridden a motorbike and twenty thousand acres of peat bog and mire is not the best place to learn. Then there was the sea trout I caught; it was the first time I had been fishing since I was a boy, and believe it or not, the one that got away was even bigger.

Fog is said to be rare on the Falklands, and even with that I was lucky, seeing it several days running. It was so thick that we were fogbound on a remote island for three days; missing the Tristar home and almost missing Badger's hedgelaying. Among those people also marooned was Norman, a 75-year-old Norfolk farmer with no teeth, on a fishing holiday, and three American travel agents. 'When I'm at t'ome an its' foggy,' Norman informed us, 'I send my ol' nephew to cler the fog. I say, git that ol' shovel and clear that ol' fog up. The other day 'e came back for dinner an' it was still foggy an' I says why en't you cleared that ol' fog away?' He said: Give me time, I en't got this far yit'. The Americans were totally bemused.

The Falklands air was also responsible for some very strange behaviour on my part. I thought that I was a confirmed and happy bachelor, but in a moment of weakness I plighted my troth – to my travelling companion, a woman. Sadly there is one deficiency on the Falklands – a shortage of engagement rings. We could not find one to fit and so she now wears a rather attractive rubber band that I found on the floor of the Upland Goose Hotel. This has one huge advantage; if lost or stolen, Eric the postman usually delivers me with a replacement six days a week.

21

Passing By

Slowly the old villagers are disappearing from the village scene. Since I attended the village school the makeup of the village has gradually changed. Then, most of the men worked in and around the village; now virtually the whole working population streams out of the parish every morning and flows back in late afternoon. Many of the old village families and names have vanished; the flexibility and mobility so admired by Tony Blair hit rural England long ago, sending village people with traditional village names looking for work and houses away from the villages where their families have lived for generations.

The old characters have gone and are going too; the passage of time inevitably finishes off what the social changes have not completed. There have been many old village characters, the squire, the blacksmith, Crabby the shepherd, 'Dut' the wart charmer and many more, all gone. I suppose I can count the remnants of the old village families on my fingers and a fortnight ago we lost one more.

She had been in the village longer than I can remember. She had apparently spent her childhood on a farm in the village High Street belonging to one of the Cambridge Colleges. It was a traditional mixed farm of that time, with cattle and cart horses, grass meadows and fields of wheat, barley, oats and tares. At the age of ten she had lost her father and the farm was run by her mother. Times were hard and the whole family had to count the pennies. Every spring while at school she had taken daffodils into Cambridge to sell for extra money and she had even sold bunches of snowdrops at school. It was a remarkable time to have a childhood, just after the First World war. She remembered airships, seeing her first car and when an aeroplane went over the harvest field it was greeted with wonder and astonishment.

Not being acquainted with the finer points of sexism and feminism she was a 'tom-boy' and enjoyed playing cricket and football with the village boys – batting left-handed and bowling right-handed. Her country childhood provided many memories, of wildflowers, larks singing and work on the farm. At the age of twelve she began courting a village boy of thirteen and when she was twenty she married him.

I first remember her when I was a small boy after the Second World War; she had progressed from being a teacher to farmer's wife. She lived in a small semi-detached farm cottage with her husband and three young children. The water was pumped by hand beyond the scullery window and the outside bucket lavatory was across a small concrete path, which must have seemed like an enormous chasm on a raw winter's night. The garden was like most country gardens at that time with daisies flowering in the lawn and a vegetable patch near the back door. There were no street lights in the village, or mains water: it seems like yesterday – it sounds like history.

Her house always seemed an incredibly happy place, the natural projection of her early romance. The exchange of love letters, sweets and stolen kisses had grown into the setting up of a home and the rearing of a family. At four feet eleven and three-quarter inches, she always seemed to have energy far in excess of her height and all day long she bustled here and there, cooking, sweeping, collecting eggs, helping with difficult calvings, singing hymns and humming. Fine old country smells were always wafting through the house, chutney, jams, pies and some-times home-made bread, and not a scrap of food was wasted. Whatever vegetable or fruit was in season, it was either in the oven or on the table.

Despite losing her father, and a brother in the Isle of Man TT races in the early 'Fifties she had an unshakeable Christian faith. She was sure that God had been good to her and her simple belief dictated that she should show her gratitude by working for Him during her mortal life. Consequently from dawn until dusk she would effervesce with religious zeal, looking after the home, teaching in the village school, doing odd jobs on the farm, taking meals to neighbours who were old or sick, and comforting those in distress. She was always in a rush, but despite her sedulity, she always made time for her children, who she believed would carry on her good work after she had departed this life; departed, she believed and hoped, to a world full of song and love, where white clad figures would teach her to play the harp.

In later life nothing seemed to change; from the farmhouse instead of the cottage she carried on as before, not seeking recognition but helping those in distress. Even in her late seventies she was visiting 'the old people', taking them flowers and cakes 'we mustn't forget them'. Her cooking too did not change and every year she would win prizes for scones, jam and rambler roses at the village flower show.

When one of her sons kicked against the system and lost his job, claiming that he wanted to write, she gave him encouragement and a roof over his head, not eviction. She had a remarkable simple philosophy of life: 'tell the truth, say what you believe and bear no grudges'. As her health failed she still served eggs at the farmhouse door. Gradually her body slowed and it was clear that the old village was going to lose another of its own. It was touch and go; she supported her second son as he stood at the recent general election and saw and enjoyed her diamond wedding day. She died at home, surrounded by her children and the Baptist church in Cambridge was packed with villagers, friends and old pupils to see her go. It was almost the end of an era – she was my mother and I shall miss her.

22

Hedgerow Hackers

A steady stream of letters continues to flow in. Yes, at this crucial time for nesting birds people are still flailing hedges and bull-dozing them up, and there seems little that can be done to stop them. As usual MAFF and the Department of the Environment seem remarkably uninterested in this annual display of legalised vandalism.

From Leicestershire comes a horrendous picture of a hedge flailed at the end of April. To say that it has been cut is an under-statement; it has been hacked, taking both height and thickness. No bird's nest could have survived the onslaught and no fledg-ling could have survived. As a landscape feature the hedge has been ruined; as an agricultural aid the hedge has been wrecked and as a wildlife refuge the hedge has been devastated. Being a roadside hedge there seems to be no logical reason for the hedge to be cut at this time of year; it seems to be a case of a farmer with nothing to do.

Gordon Beningfield, the CRT's Vice-Chairman recently got into hot water for saying exactly this. He said: 'Some farmers leave me almost speechless. They call themselves "Guardians of the Countryside" and then smash up hedges in the summer, simply because they can think of nothing else to do'. For his trouble he had an irate farmer on the phone for over three quarters of an hour. Mr Angry explained everything except why some farmers feel the need to cut their hedges when the birds are nesting. If any hedge-cutting hooligan farmer, or the NFU can explain summer hedge-cutting I will be happy to report their views.

The old Government's tired and long overdue legislation to save a few hedgerows in each parish is set to become law on July

1st. To celebrate the occasion, reports are still coming in from all over lowland England of farmers grubbing up hedges likely to be covered by the legislation 'to beat the Bill'.

Farmers are not alone of course. Developers are still doing their bit to flatten hedges ideal for breeding birds. Close to the famous Trinity Foot Public House, off the A14 between Huntingdon and Cambridge is a field in the middle of open countryside. The land was once owned by a District Councillor and, hey-ho, suddenly the field of this community spirited landowner became ideal for industrial development – to create jobs, etc, of course. District and Parish councillors with land are a very public spirited section of the community – I have seen it happen so often – land that looks most unlikely for development, suddenly getting planning permission, for 'the good of the community' – it is all rather heart-warming.

The land in question stood neglected for several years, and now, in the middle of the nesting season the luxuriant roadside hedge has been flattened. Fortunately it appears to be nobody's fault. The Civil Engineers, Breheny of Downham Market, claim that they are simply obeying instructions, and those who know the reason for the summer work at January's, the agents, are always 'in a meeting' and seem unable to phone back. Nobody, it appears, is accountable.

Because of this destruction and as part of the Save Our Hedges Campaign, the CRT has now written to the new Secretary of State for the Environment, Mr John Prescott, asking him to protect hedgerows during the summer breeding season. He has been asked to amend the Wildlife and Countryside Act to protect hedges from the flail-mower and bulldozer between April 1st and July 31st. It will be interesting to see if the new Labour Government has any more commitment than the old clapped-out Tory one – it would be impossible to have less.

The hedgerow saga is not all gloom and doom. The hedge laid by Badger in early March is looking a picture. It has nearly all survived his chainsaw and axe and in another year it will actually be stock proof. It looks too as if Badger's skills will be passed on. The CRT recently announced a day's introduction to hedge-laying by the redoubtable Badger – it was oversubscribed within a week.

The stretch of hedge cut by a Bomford mower in mid-March is also looking good, showing that a hedge can be flailed sensibly and responsibly at the right time of the year. One of the arguments against late cutting on arable land is that 'it will damage the crop'. In March, we deliberately ran over the crop with the tractor and hedge-cutter. The wheat concerned already looks the same as the rest of the field and this part of the crop is to be combined with a special combine, which weighs the yield exactly, to compare it with a strip not run over by the hedge-cutter – we will then be able to see if the crop was damaged.

I have just watched a remarkable video. It is of a BBC television programme first shown in 1972. Called the 'The Vanishing Hedgerows' it is presented by Henry Williamson of *Tarka the Otter* fame, and produced by David Cobham. In it, Henry Williamson is using the arguments we are still using today. He warns of the loss of the English partridge; he is astonished and saddened by farmers actually spraying under their hedges to get rid of the wildflowers, 'weeds to the robot-minded'. Much of it is filmed on Williamson's old farm at Stiffkey in Norfolk and the wildlife photography is stunning. Why can't the BBC, or anybody else for that matter, make personalised wildlife programmes of this quality today?

23

The Trap

———

Politicians are not known for their sense of humour, but just lately whenever I have felt depressed and in need of a good laugh I have turned to the Labour Party's Election Manifesto,

'New Labour Because Britain Deserves Better'. There on page 31 I read 'Labour aims to reform the Common Agricultural Policy to save money, to support the rural economy and enhance the environment' – ho, ho, ho. Over recent weeks I have been to various conferences and launches where that wonderful double act of Michael Meacher and Elliott Morley have repeated the joke with such success that various conservation bodies have also taken up the theme – conservation in England, Britain and the whole of Europe will take a huge step forward 'when the CAP is reformed'. Their main policies depend on a reform that will not happen in the foreseeable future and so all the words, spoken and printed about the environment after 'CAP Reform' are straight from Cloud Cuckoo Land.

Like the Conservatives before them the Labour Government is drifting in a fantasy world in which they believe they have an influence on European agricultural policy. Poor John Seldom Glummer was under the same illusion and all the Conservatives managed to do in eighteen years was to make the situation even worse and the plight of farmland, wildlife, and traditional farming families critical.

The recent changes in the CAP were given much advance publicity and the world 'reform' was used with gay, or even light-hearted abandon. The mixture was the same as before. Payments would reduce slightly, in theory, but with set-aside disappearing and various adjustments to subsidies the amount of money available, paid for by the taxpayer, will actually rise.

Proof that the changes mean very little comes from the welcome given to them by the NFU. So the organisation that appears to be run by and for the top 20% elite of British farming is satisfied. And where are the great environmental reforms? There aren't any. In fact with the disappearance of compulsory set-aside the grey partridge, the brown hare, the skylark and the lapwing will again by under pressure. At least set-aside gave them brief respite and numbers have improved in some areas as a direct result.

The Government's sense of humour was shown once more at the Royal Show. Again, New Labour boasts a 'green' image and 'green' intent and claims to want to 'enhance the environment' through CAP reform. In that case why did the Department of Trade and Industry have a stand at the Royal Show urging and encouraging farmers to go into Eastern Europe? Such a movement will take the worst of our industrial farming into the vast environmentally rich areas of Hungary, Poland and the Czech Republic. It seems a case of the Left hand – the DTI (Margaret Beckett), not Knowing what the Right hand – MAFF and the Department of the Environment (Messrs Prescott and Cunningham) is doing or saying. Some people would call the muddle a 'lack of co-ordination'; hypocrisy seems to be a more accurate description.

The DTI seminars were brimming over with smooth-handed Savile-Row-suited gentlemen calling themselves 'farmers', all anxious to get over to Eastern Europe with good soils, cheap land and cheaper labour. It seems of little interest to these prophets of profit and 'maximum efficiency' that their activities could be the beginning of the end for the great bustard, the corncrake, the lesser kestrel, the aquatic warbler, the black stork, the white stork, and others. The havoc caused to the wildlife and rural communities of Western Europe is now going to be heaped onto Eastern Europe; the lessons that should have been learnt from the industrialisation of British agriculture are still being ignored and New Labour is actually encouraging the export of old environmental devastation.

Regrettably in Hungary that devastation has already started. One British consortium, 'Bihar '96' has purchased 15,000 acres in the Bihar region of Hungary, including some prime habitat of the great bustard – one of Europe's rarest birds. For years I have been a fan of the great bustard, indeed it was once a bird of my part of England, but sadly it now remains only in assorted Coats of Arms for Cambridgeshire. It seems incredible that after making the poor bird extinct in Britain, British farmers are now going to do their bit to put pressure on the great bustard in Hungary.

Already 1200 acres have been ruined for the bustard by ploughing and direct drilling and incredibly the consortium is asking for compensation, at twenty times the Hungarian rate, to stop them cultivating the rest. Obviously our British 'Guardians of the Countryside' now wish to export their form of guardianship on an unsuspecting, almost innocent part of Europe. If the Labour Government is as 'green' as it claims to be, then surely it must take action; let's hope that the RSPB's Chief Executive, Barbara Young, one of Labour's newly created peers, can kick them into action – perhaps she could even become Baroness Bustard of Bihar.

The truth is that Britain is caught in the CAP; outvoted by countries doing well financially out of the system and uninterested in the resulting environmental damage or consequences. In other words we are trapped. It is hardly surprising that Sir James Goldsmith's great exposé of the EU and GATT was called 'The Trap'. The death of Sir James hit me hard on a personal and political level. The Grim Reaper has been hyperactive in my life this last nine months. It was after reading 'The Trap' that I became interested in the Referendum Party. A meeting with Sir James convinced me that the only way to try to change the CAP and the equally destructive Common Fisheries Policy was by political action. When I met him I expected to meet a dominating autocrat. Instead I met a man of insight and intellect with a wicked sense of humour. Although my Methodist and Baptist forbears would have not approved of every aspect of his life, here was a man doing what he thought was right. Originally he wanted me to stand against John Major, but my favouring my home constituency was not a problem to him.

It is now obvious that his participation in the election was an act of great courage. People asked 'what are his motives'? He had no motives, apart from doing what needed to be done; he was already a dying man. The day before the election he flew to the farm and met our local supporters, and had a special word for my old father. Throughout the last exciting year he treated me with great kindness and friendship, and I feel proud to have been involved with his election campaign. Grown men don't cry, but this particular peasant is growing used to shedding tears.

24

The Golden Hoof

———

For years I have been puzzled: whenever sheep, shepherds and sheepdogs are mentioned in ordinary conversation, they seem to be linked automatically with the Lake District, Scotland and Wales, as if the sheep-based traditions of the rest of Britain are an irrelevance. Consequently the old shepherds and their sheep in Kent, Dorset, the Cotswolds and East Anglia etc have all been forgotten; instead we link sheep with 'One Man and His Dog' and a hillside in the Lakes.

Of course the shepherds of Britain's hill country are a tough skilled breed, but the shepherding traditions in the rest of the country are just as important. Because of this I was pleased that the English National Sheep Dog Trials have just been held in East Anglia for the first time. Sheep were a vital part of the East Anglian economy for generations and became the 'golden hoof' in the famous Norfolk four course rotation.

It was most appropriate too that the trials took place within the grounds of Holkham Hall, where the present Earl, Lord Leicester, still has sheep in his farming rotation, just like his famous farming ancestor, Thomas Coke (pronounced 'Cook') of Holkham.

The Trials were well run and the setting was perfect around the great house and lake set in mature parkland. The standard was incredibly high and Britain's shepherds and sheep dogs must be the best in the world. Sadly we will never know as our top trial-lists are still not allowed to take their dogs abroad to compete, without having to make them suffer the absurd six months in quarantine afterwards. With sheep dog trialling gaining in popularity in the USA, Australia, New Zealand, South Africa, the

Falklands and mainland Europe, it is absurd that British sheep-dogs can only compete against other British sheepdogs. With good anti-rabies vaccines available it surely is time that the Government did something about the present antiquated system. The inert Tory Government sat on the problem for long enough; it must be hoped that the new government actually does something.

The position is made more ridiculous by the fact that horses can contract rabies, just as easily as dogs, yet racehorses, show jumpers, eventers, etc, are all allowed to travel the world competing, while our border collies are forced to stay at home. When common sense eventually prevails and our shepherds and handlers can travel abroad I think it will quickly be proved that British border collies really are the best in the world.

The ever increasing popularity of sheep dog trialling was shown at Holkham by the large number of Belgians, Swedes and Dutch who had made the trip to England specifically to see 'The English National'. What was even more alarming was the number who approached me with the words: 'Hallow Misster Parge vee haf been vatching you on television'. Apparently 'One Man and His Dog' is available on European cable TV and is very popular; what an honour to be part of Britain's export industry.

Sadly, although sheep dog trials and 'One Man and His Dog' are increasingly popular abroad, their popularity at home seems to be on the wane. I understand that the next series of 'One Man and His Dog' on BBC 2 will be the last series to feature the 'Young Handlers Competition'. Regrettably, although much of the broadcast media's output seems aimed at 'yoof culture', civilised, sensible country youth are to be ignored. It seems to be yet another indication that the rural community is becoming an increasingly ignored minority in its own country. For me, presenting 'Young Handlers' has been a highlight of 'One Man and His Dog'; it has been a way to encourage young people to come into the sport, and also to get those youngsters already handling dogs to improve their skills. Sadly it seems that the BBC would rather have young country shepherds playing computer games or watching the Spice Girls mime on Top of the Pops. Clearly its programme planning is based on an urban, current affairs view of life in Britain, and those with a rural outlook are gradually being excluded.

It was ironic that at Holkham I was introduced to a ten-year-old young man, Edward Hawkens, whose main ambition in life is to get a sheep dog and compete in Young Handlers – sadly I hadn't the heart to tell him of reality. He comes from a totally non-farming background but has become absorbed by the skill involved in trialling, and by the special relationship that builds up between man and dog. He goes to watch sheep dog trials at every opportunity, and the arrival of the National Championships was a special bonus to him. He has a beautiful carved crook, and now all he wants is a dog. Fortunately Sarah Jenkins, one of the East Anglia's most accomplished triallers, has taken him under her wing, and who knows, if the BBC can be persuaded that all sections of the community should be served, perhaps the Corporation can reinstate Young Handlers with the Spice Girls presenting the prizes – that way everybody will be satisfied.

There were a large number of splendidly carved crooks and sticks at the trials. Incredibly, traditional stick making is another country tradition under threat. Many of the best sticks have handles carved from ram's horn. Unbelievably, due to the present BSE, CJD, Scrapie scares, all ram's horn now has to be destroyed as a 'specified risk material'. What nonsense; I have a ram's horn crook, I walk with it, I don't suck it or chew it; what we really, really want is protection from Mad scientist, politician, bureaucrat and broadcaster disease.

25

Muddy Waters

This year the village pond has undergone a transformation. For years it has been the centre of controversy: some have said 'clean it out', others have cried 'fill it in'. It has been described as an object of great beauty, and accused of being a major health hazard. As a result it has led to the Annual Parish Meeting running into extra time on several occasions. The pond itself stands in almost the centre of the old village where the water table is at its highest. No doubt at one time it was just a wet hollow where water stood throughout the year.

In the age of real horsepower, carts were driven through the pond to clean their wheels, a routine that had finished by my school days. Then, in the summer it held all three types of British newt in large numbers, the common, the palmate and the now endangered great crested. In winter it became the centre for winter sports, where a slide would be made from one side almost to the other.

Over the years the pond went into decline. Gradually the newts disappeared; ducks arrived and the water never cleared. Various theories were put forward; filthy water from the nearby road caused pollution; the stream providing most of its flow had been secretly diverted and silt from a ditch had filled it up. I must confess that I thought the problems were caused by a combination of all three. Consequently, when a suggestion was made to 'clear the pond out' I believed that all the hard labour would make no difference; the silt, pollution and the ducks would still win.

In the spring a local farmer and the parish clerk quite literally got stuck into the problem. Most people, myself included, watched on in knowing amazement, ready to say 'I told you so' as soon as the work finished and the pond immediately resumed its old dirty appearance. How wrong we prophets of doom were. The water is now too deep for the ducks to tip up and churn up the bottom and the water is almost crystal clear. If it stays this way and the water is still clear next spring, perhaps newts can even be helped back. There is a danger in the return of newts of course; the pond is also near one of the village pubs. It would be a tragedy for late night human newts to join the real things in the now deep water.

The village post office and stores stands directly next to the pond. At a time when there is concern throughout the country over the future of village shops and post offices, it is depressing to find that Tescos have put on a free bus service that picks up customers directly outside the village shop, to cart them several miles away to one of its superstores. Unfortunately most supermarkets can sell their produce cheaper than the local shop can buy it – hardly the principle on which to base fair competition.

The attitude of the supermarkets is difficult to follow. A few days ago I went to a launch of an exciting scheme to save the skylark, in which Tescos were busy clambering all over the RSPB. On the surface everything seemed fine, apart from the continued use of the word 'sustainable'.

Surely a system that is 'sustainable' is not just about skylarks, it is about the people who live and work in the countryside too, and it should be about trying to make thriving and viable rural communities? One sure way to damage a rural community and help it to become unviable is by putting at risk its village shop and post office with what appears to be unfair competition. If Tescos really want 'sustainability' in the countryside then surely its suited PR men should be considering the needs of the whole countryside – skylarks, family farms and villages? Instead of taking custom away from local village shops, why can't the supermarkets sell a wide range of their products cheaply to village shops for resale? By so doing they would still be making a profit and showing concern for the long term future of the whole countryside.

The many letters and messages I have received from readers concerning the loss of my mother have been heart-warming. Several letters made an interesting point; how the writers moved into villages from towns, to be made welcome by villagers of my mother's generation. From the old villagers they learnt about the past which made them understand the present; it has allowed them to feel close to their new communities and feel real 'country people'. Sir Laurens van der Post always maintained that 'the city mind' could be changed through the right contact with the countryside and nature. It is good to know that the fading generation is still helping this process to take place. Interestingly too, Sir Laurens also believed that it was possible to have a 'country mind' while living in the city. It is all a matter of attitude, perception and appreciation.

The recent heavy rain, although much needed has been a disaster for young birds. Numerous broods have been wiped out. Astonishingly one family of blackbirds has survived. The CRT's tenant farmer, Tim Scott, noticed that after he parked his Daihatsu Fourtrak in the yard, a blackbird flew backwards and forwards in quick succession. He looked underneath his vehicle to find a blackbird's nest on the chassis, with youngsters about to fledge. Over recent days they have travelled miles. The question is, did the mother also travel miles while incubating? The Daihatsu has now been parked until the young birds fly.

26

Mad Mowers and Flailers

———

Harvest is over and I am thankful. In the middle of May it looked as if we were heading for a disaster; the drought had set in and it seemed to me that another 1976 weather pattern was established. The grass had already stopped growing and I could not see how all the cereal crops could survive. Then came the wet June, and there is no doubt that it did spoil Wimbledon, but it did quite literally save our bacon and our beer.

To show their appreciation for the saved harvest there are now numerous farmers throughout the country mowing their hedges, to ensure that the harvest of the hedgerow cannot, and will not be enjoyed by man, bird and beast. Hips, haws, sloes and black-berries are being shredded, as are the potential shoots for next year's berries. The farmers have got their crops and subsidies, the redwings and fieldfares of winter can look after themselves. It is short-sighted, ignorant 'land-management', it cannot be called farming. Farming is about responsibility and working with nature; hedge-cutting at this time of year, and every year, is about irresponsibility and working against nature.

The usual argument by the flailers and mowers is that to cut hedges later in the year, after the berries have been eaten, would involve running over the growing new crop, which would damage it and lead to a reduced yield at harvest time. To me it always did seem to be a flawed argument as in the old days flocks of sheep actually grazed on winter wheat in the spring, with no detrimental effect on the yield. In addition of course cereal crops are rolled in the spring – they are not damaged by it, but improved by it – so why should a tractor with a hedge-cutter attached damage the crop?

Because of this, the Countryside Restoration Trust deliberately cut a length of hedgerow in early March. Not only was the length of hedgerow cut, but Bomfords, the mower manufacturers, were asked to show no concern for the crop. Half the hedge was cut and half the hedge was left uncut and the winter wheat on both sections was otherwise treated in exactly the same way. Being 'headland', where the tractor turns during ploughing, the yield is always slightly down on the rest of the field. Consequently by harvest I expected both strips of wheat to yield almost identi-cally, and I was willing to accept a slight drop in yield where the hedge-cutting had taken place.

As soon as the wheat was ripe a special combine arrived,

provided and operated by Novartis Crop Protection, and so the cutting and monitoring was carried out with total independence. Three cuts were taken alongside both sections of the hedge showing a yield of almost two tons an acre on one strip and $2\frac{1}{2}$ tons on the other. The highest yield was where the hedge-cutting had taken place – so much for the argument 'we can't cut the hedge later in the year, it will damage the crop'.

There is even a simple explanation for the increased yield. When the crop is trampled and torn, it 'tillers' (throws out additional shoots) more easily. So our 'Save Our Hedges Campaign' has already flattened one argument put out by the mad hedge-cutting brigade. The truth is that hedge-cutting is done at the wrong time of the year because the land-owners can think of nothing better to do; they are more concerned with tidiness and farming fashion than with fostering and encouraging a living countryside.

Sadly I have been receiving a steady stream of letters through-out the summer reporting hedges being cut all over the country, even during the key bird breeding months of May, June and July. One of the worst incidents occurred in Colchester, not involving a farmer, but Colchester Borough Council. Unbelievably the Council cut a hedge around a recreation ground in June. Mrs Jean Devall found dead and dying birds after the cutter had passed by; 'I picked up one little bird that was still alive but they had been mutilated. Those in the first nest had feathers, and perhaps in another week they could have been flying'.

Colchester Borough Council's reaction to her was incredible: 'We cannot delay the work any further and you must admit that this particular hedge was overgrown and untidy looking'. Most urban people and councils are against fox hunting; evidently Colchester Council are not against shredding birds alive.

By cutting when they did the Borough Council almost certainly broke the Wildlife and Countryside Act, but neither the Council nor the Colchester Police seem interested. The Council claims that the hedge was inspected for birds' nests, showing an awareness of the provisions of the Act, but they still went ahead in the breeding season. When I asked the Colchester Police why no action had been taken I was first put on to an Inspector Finch; unfortunately he had flown away on holiday and I was but on to another Inspector; he seemed totally uninterested in 'birds' nests', and even sounded annoyed that I should have wasted his time. He promised to ring back with information about the case – he never did. What is the point of having an Act to protect breeding birds if the police have neither the understanding, expertise, nor interest to implement the law?

27

The Volvette and the Damselfly

———

Will I get through this chapter and stay awake, that is the question; I feel exhausted. Yes I am busy; yes I have been carting bales, but my fatigue is totally unconnected with work. The truth is that I am on yet another crash diet. The need to slim is quite simple and I have virtually stopped eating. My problem became apparent when I tried my 'One Man and His Dog' trousers on, as filming is about to start again. My smart clothes came out for their annual airing and I tried the trousers on; I could not do one pair up – by at least three inches. So my choice was stark; stop eating and reduce the waist line, buy new larger trousers, or present 'One Man and His Dog' wearing wellington boots, a smart jacket and no trousers at all. A diet seemed the most sensible solution and if anybody wants to follow suit and lose a pound a day this is the self-inflicted nightmare that I would recommend; for breakfast three damsons and a cup of tea; dinner, a beetroot sandwich and tea, an apple. Weight is falling off, but will I survive?

I don't normally put weight on in the summer but this summer has been different. With all the turmoil in my life I suppose I have been stress-eating. It is a myth of course, that our summer diet is healthy and low in calories; lashings of salad cream, pork pies, strawberries and cream, and ice cream quickly dispose of that argument.

The other day I achieved a first, I had to go to the Black Hole, and these days I travel from Cambridge station, to prevent my Daihatsu from being stolen or dismantled by the Royston didecoys. Travelling in to Cambridge is a major problem however, during school term time, as the roads are choked by streams of 'Volvettes'. A Volvette is the highly manicured driver of a Volvo estate, taking Julian and Jasmine 'in to town to school', causing massive traffic chaos as a direct result. If all these children travelled by bus or train and the Volvettes stayed at home, half the new by-passes in Britain would not be needed. Consequently, I left early and reached the station with half an hour to spare; so I sat down and happily read a fascinating article on the current status of the otter. So fascinating was it, that as I read the train came in, waited for a quarter of an hour and left the platform just as I looked up.

One of these days I must sit down by the brook and wait for otters. Otter activity has been remarkable lately with as many as four spraints appearing in a single night. It seems to indicate that a bitch and cubs are using the area regularly. Every day I water my sheep using a high-tech bucket tied to a piece of bailer-twine to get water from the brook; I go at irregular times and on each occasion the thought occurs that this may be the day when I meet an otter, but so far I have been out of luck.

It is surprising what coincides with these daily visits and I must meet face to face with an otter one day. The most amazing day for me was a few weeks ago when the banded demoiselle damsel flies were flying. They are astonishingly beautiful and the sun on their silky banded wings makes them glow.

I had never stopped to watch these amazing creatures mate before. I had assumed that they would be like other dragonflies or damsel flies, laying their eggs from the surface, or even sprinkling them at random. The day I stopped to watch I could not believe what I saw. The female landed on a floating reed and then with her wings closed she walked down the stalk and under water, until she was so deep that she disappeared from view. I was astonished, previously I had simply never stopped to see this incredible procedure. Apparently they can stay under water for up to two hours.

The other pleasure over recent weeks at the water's edge has been the reed buntings in the reeds. For twenty years they have been absent in the summer. Last year one pair returned to breed and this year there have been at least four. The habitat has come back and with it has come this attractive little bird.

28

The Bird They All Forgot

———

Each day I scan the skies for the return of friends, but so far the air is empty. Just a few years ago odd groups of lapwings appeared towards the end of July, but now their return becomes later and later. Last year it was well into September before they returned and yet again numbers are visibly down.

The decline of the lapwing, green plover or 'peewit', is a sad tale, although there are some signs of hope. It is one of the most beautiful birds, but somehow its decline seems to have been forgotten and its plight overlooked. In winter or summer the sight or sound of the lapwing is evocative of space, sky and traditional countryside. Once it was a bird of highland and lowland, wetland, valley, meadow and moor. Now it is a bird in retreat; each year its numbers fall still more, a collapse that has meant a decline of over 50% in just twenty years (and 65% in the last thirty years). The British Trust for Ornithology believes that numbers could be down to as few as 120,000 pairs with great swathes of lowland England now without breeding lapwings.

For me the battle for the lapwing is every bit as important as the fight to save the skylark. It seems incredible that up to twenty years ago the lapwing was a common bird of winter and summer in my part of lowland Britain. In the two decades since, it has ceased to breed in my parish, and most of the neighbouring ones, and it has become only a winter visitor. Lapwings were one of the first signs of spring before their decline, tumbling in display over the water meadows now owned by the CRT. Then their usual 'peewit' call became a piping cascade of notes every bit as attractive and erratic as their flight. In the cereal fields too the 'peewits' nested, on bare earth, and in the spring corn. As my father cultivated, or rolled the land, he would put a stick in the ground at each nest so he could avoid them. On plough land all four dark, mottled eggs would be moved onto a fresh furrow, so that ploughing could continue. Soon the hen bird would return to resume incubation on her newly sited nest.

Later lapwing chicks and adolescents were a common sight, and gradually as the summer moved on several family groups would merge into small flocks. With autumn and winter more birds would arrive from the north and huge flocks would follow the plough. At autumn dusk, in the bronze light of the setting sun, nothing was more beautiful than a peewit with its bright white breast shining against the rich green sheen of its wings and crested head. As more birds came in it was always so easy to see why they were named 'lapwings'. They were part of my countryside, an integral part of the country year – they belonged.

In those days of huge winter flocks and musical spring meadows, who could have guessed that the lapwing would soon be in danger? It is the old, old, story; 'efficient', industrialised farming has left no space for the lapwing. Habitat has been destroyed, or in the parlance of the agri-businessman, 'improved'; many pesticides have proved to be distinctly lapwing unfriendly and predators have increasingly targeted those birds that have managed to survive. Now my summers never see a lapwing and even the winter flocks have shrunk to a fraction of their former size. The lapwing is in crisis, but with political action, and commonsense farming, it can be brought back from the brink.

Without a doubt many of the problems faced by the lapwing have been created by the Common Agricultural Policy. Production has been driven upwards by subsidies, and the means of production and their effect on the countryside and its wildlife seem to have been of little account. In lowland Britain the emphasis has been on increasing arable production based on greater intensification and relying on chemical 'inputs' – artificial fertilisers, herbicides and pesticides. Lapwings have not been considered as an 'output'.

Lapwings like to nest on almost open ground or in short crops, consequently the switch to a rotation based on winter sown wheat, barley and rape has meant that the vegetation is often too high and lush to allow the birds to nest. In addition the sprays can remove insects for both young and adult birds alike and the spraying of some toxic chemicals can lead directly to lapwing deaths. The move to greater intensification and more widespread arable farming has been fuelled by EU subsidies.

Sadly the intensification and industrialisation of agriculture has spread to livestock farming too, and this is proving to be just as destructive to the lapwing. Each year more and more grass-land is cut for silage so that cattle can be kept more intensively (sometimes kept indoors throughout the year to maximise grass production), and cutting is carried out in the key nesting months of April, May and June. Eggs are smashed and young birds are shredded. Some of the cutters travel as fast as a man can run, and cut down to almost ground level – the young birds, and even the adults stand absolutely no chance. Incredibly, one of the culprits is the National Trust; evidently chasing a single deer or fox is considered evil – mincing ground-nesting birds such as the lapwing, skylark and partridge through the irresponsible use of grass is regarded as 'good husbandry'.

Throughout Britain pasture is being 'improved'. Once rough fields with water flushes and patches of rush are being drained, sprayed and re-seeded. The most common sight in sheepland is not the shepherd, but the Hymac driver, draining, and spraying the rushes surrounding his new drains. It is a depressing sight for these were the areas favoured by lapwing, curlew, snipe and redshank. A gamekeeper in Cheshire recently said to me: 'What's happening is a tragedy. If it keeps going on like this the lapwing and the curlew will be gone. Some farmers are just greedy and some large landowners don't realise what their farm managers are up to'.

The reason for the change is simple – improved grass means more sheep per acre, providing a subsidy from £19.50 per ewe in lowland England, to £31.74 in the most disadvantaged highland areas. The money is so good that it recently led to a headline in *Farmers Weekly* proclaiming 'Rough land re-seed cost recouped in only a year'. Since the commencement of the EU Sheepmeat Regime in October 1980 the sheep population of Britain has risen by almost 40% to 41.5 million – the lapwing decrease has been just as spectacular. In the same period sheep subsidies have risen from a total of £42 million to nearly £422 million – many times greater than conservation payments in sheep areas. It has helped Britain's export trade; fuelled the export of live sheep scandal and led to over-stocking, over-grazing and the trampling of nests in many of the most beautiful parts of Britain. It is also leading to a wildlife calamity as numbers of lapwings, skylarks and curlews plummet. The calamity is not just limited to improved grassland, for even on rough grass and moorland, some farmers are rolling and harrowing the grass at peak nesting time, in order to get just a fraction more grazing for one more sheep. Lindsay Waddell, Chairman of the Moorland Gamekeepers Association, and former Council Member of English Nature says: 'We must be found to be supporting the rural community without damaging the environment and there is no doubt that headage payments have done just that. Therefore another system must be sought'.

It is vital that before it is too late these subsidies become 'farm' subsidies, based on the needs of a family farm and sympathetic husbandry, not on 'headage' payments based on over-grazing and destroying the land. At the moment the average family hill farm makes a profit of just £14,500, after receiving subsidies of £19,700. Subsidies are essential to keep our hill country alive, but it is equally important that they are redirected to ensure that the hills are alive with the sound of curlews, lapwings and larks, as well as sheep and shepherds.

The total production subsidies to British farming exceed £3b per year with only a paltry £100m going to environmentally friendly farming schemes. The result is plummeting wildlife, that if unchecked will see the virtual disappearance of the lapwing within a decade. The only hope is urgent CAP reform linking subsidies with the environment. As Graham Wynne, Director of Conservation for the RSPB says: 'CAP promises production at the expense of the environment. Radical reform is long overdue and Jack Cunningham should take a lead in Europe which has reward for Environmentally Sensitive farming at its heart'.

Inevitably the industrialisation of cereal and livestock farming has led to a number of chemicals being commonly used that create yet more problems for the beleaguered lapwing. Some pesticides are poisoning the insects, molluscs and crustaceans on which the lapwing depends for food, others are killing the vegetation the insects themselves need for survival, and some of the chemical cocktails are actually poisoning the lapwings directly. Among those contributing to the crisis are thought to be fonofos – an organophosphorus insecticide, metaldehyde, sodium monochloroacetate, etc.

So, on arable land the lapwing is having its food source removed and it is being poisoned. Another problem is the speed at which land is now ploughed. My old father points out that in the old days with a horse, one acre a day would be ploughed by a good ploughman and his horse. This gave the lapwing many days of good feeding. Now, with fewer invertebrates in the soil, a large tractor can plough 20 acres a day and so the days when the lapwing flocks can feed on freshly turned soil are few and far between. Around here this year many fields of winter barley were harvested and ploughed in July. When the lapwings eventually return these areas will already be foodless.

As lapwing numbers fall so predator numbers are rising steadily, and predation has become one more important factor in the decline of the lapwing. As populations decline, so defence mechanisms, such as rising up in unison at the approach of a crow, become less effective. The particular problems are magpies, crows and foxes, all of which are experiencing population explosions. The crow population has trebled since 1962 and the magpie population has doubled; the increase in fox numbers seems to have been even greater. For many years all three were persecuted in country areas, by gamekeepers and all those with free-range hens. In my village during my childhood every other house had hens and so foxes, crows and magpies were rarities. Now most people buy their battery eggs from supermarkets, gamekeeping has declined and the destructive three have few enemies. In the past too, numbers of foxes, crows and magpies were controlled naturally by lack of food in winter; now with plenty of fresh meat as road kills, winter bird tables and food put out for livestock, they have never had it so good. The problem is confirmed by the RSPB in its excellent report 'Silent Fields' published in 1995. The report shows quite clearly that due to predation by crows, magpies and foxes, the lapwing and curlew populations of Northern Ireland and Wales are not sustainable. Many naturalists believe that a similar situation exists in England and Scotland.

Last year the RSPB carried out a survey of bird populations in the Pennines on land where gamekeepers controlled pedators, and land with no control. The conclusions have not yet been published but they are said to confirm the earlier work in Wales and Ireland.

In 1988 Dr David Baines, a research ecologist with the Game Conservancy gained his PhD with a study of the lapwing. Last year he returned to four of his study areas. In the Eden Valley, where there had been no predator control on two areas, lapwing numbers had fallen drastically from 110 pairs to 23 pairs and from 80 pairs to just 12. By comparison two areas in Teesdale with gamekeepers showed an entirely different picture. On one, lapwing numbers had increased from 25 pairs to 40 and on the other they had remained constant at 45. Dr Baines is convinced that outside game areas the outlook for the lapwing is gloomy.

Because of the threat to the lapwing I have phoned a number of farmers throughout East Anglia to ask after their lapwing populations. Most lost their birds years ago and those still with breeding pairs talk of numbers falling to critical levels.

There are however two significant exceptions. The first is Christ Knights. He is a remarkable man; his farm in the Norfolk Brecks was started by his grandfather – born in a converted henhouse, and now extends to some 9000 acres. Not only does he run a highly intensive and productive farm, supplying parsnips, carrots and iceburg lettuces to most of the supermarkets, but with almost 10% of his land left in grass margins and conservation areas, plus control of crows, magpies and foxes, he has a farm teeming with wildlife. His lapwing population is growing slowly and he has the largest concentration of ground-nesting stone curlews in the country – ideal for his other activity – wildlife film-making for Anglia's 'Survival' programme. On one block of 2000 acres he has managed to increase the number of lapwing nests from 'Five or six five years ago, to forty pairs this year'. He believes that the secret lies in providing the right habitat, predator control and encouraging his tractor drivers to look out for them. 'We're showing our tractor drivers where to look for nests and how to find them. Lapwing nests are easy to find in a field. The old drivers have been doing this for years, but now we have some youngsters coming along, they are doing very well and becoming very keen'.

Peter Wombwell farms on the Cambridgeshire/Essex border and he too has breeding lapwings in an area where most of the summer birds disappeared years ago. As a set-aside option he has used fifty acres to recreate chalk grassland with patches of bare fallow. In the very first year, three years ago, three pairs of lapwings returned and bred; last year there were six and this year, seven. Three of the nests were monitored this summer by the RSPB and each successfully brought off three young. At present they have been joined by a flock of between 30–40 birds. Sian Wombwell, guarding the phone while her husband is at harvest is proud of what has happened: 'On this farm every acre has to work, but we want wildlife as well, and there is so much scope for conservation. I feel that many farmers simply give a passing nod to conservation. Unless we do more it will be too late'. The ideal form of management for the Wombwells' fifty acres of chalk grassland would be to run a few sheep on the land – thus creating ideal lapwing habitat. Incredibly MAFF interprets set-aside rules so strictly that sheep are not allowed, instead Peter Wombwell has had to get a cutter, to mow the area in strips, trying to mimic sheep grazing.

Again, one of the most significant aspects of this positive lapwing story is predator control. Peter Wombwell again controls crows, magpies and foxes in the spring – aimed at control not extinction. It is a case of habitat management with population management – when are some conservation bodies going to learn that the two go hand in hand?

29

Proud to be a Nimby

In the living language of the Peoples' Cool Britannia, it is most 'uncool' to be a NIMBY. At a time when environmentally illiterate politicians, ego tripping local councillors and get-rich quick developers are spinning the myth that 4.4 million new houses, or even 5.5 million, are urgently needed, many of them in the open countryside, those of us who proclaim 'NOT IN MY BACK YARD' are depicted as selfish, 'I'm alright Jack' individuals determined to keep others away from our rural paradise. Indeed even some NIMBIES themselves are apologetic about their stance, brainwashed into feelings of shame and guilt, for a moral position that is in fact heroic.

I am proud to be a NIMBY, and not only am I proud to be a NIMBY, but I am also glad to be a NOTE – Not Over There Either, and euphoric about being considered a BANANA – Build

Absolutely Nothing Anywhere Near Anywhere. In other words – sorry, the countryside is full.

No doubt some people will claim that I take this position simply because I do not have any land to develop myself. Sorry – wrong there too. If we wanted to play the planning game in the same way as many other people and institutions, we would claim that our farmyard was redundant and sell its two or three acres as prime building land for at least £1m. Unfortunately I believe the system is wrong and the whole concept of 4.4 million more houses in the countryside is both indefensible and unsustainable. I would rather be honest and poor, than sell-out my country heritage for the developer's thirty pieces of silver.

In addition, of course, not only should the current development-mania be seen as an attack on the Green Belt – the countryside – it is also an attack on country people themselves; a minority whose livelihoods and lifestyles are being assaulted from all sides. Apparently rural culture is only welcome in other overseas countries – it is not welcome in 'multi-cultural' Britain.

The message is simple; if people really want to live in the countryside, then wait your turn. If all you want is a replica of suburbia built in the country – get your urban politicians to clean up your own back yard and build on the thousands of wasted, neglected acres there. Sadly, the simple truth is that urban and municipal authorities do not want to build houses, it is more remunerative to go for business parks and industrial areas with their high yielding business rates, while the commuting work force can queue to get into town during the morning and queue to get out at night. Then too, VAT is chargeable on restoring dilapidation, while new build is VAT free. It is madness. Planning? It is planning chaos.

The irony of the current situation is that the intention to steal vast swathes of the Green Belt came immediately after the Secretary of State for the Environment, Mr John Prescott, had been regailing the nations of the world, gathered in Japan, to have regard for their environment. The buzz word was 'sustainability'. As soon as he returned home he announced his plans for the Green Belt, showing that not only did he fail to understand the world 'environment', but that he did not understand the meaning of 'sustainability' either. In its Manifesto, New Labour commits itself to Green policies, the environment and the countryside; in practice New Labour is no different from discredited Old T in other words: Tony Blair = Hot Air.

d Tories became too apoplectic about Labour's Green B hey should remember that as in so many political are vs, New Labour's policy is only a continuation of Old v. What John Prescott is apparently so keen to finish d by none other than John Seldom Glummer.

Fou million houses do not just simply mean stolen land, t nore roads, more waste, more noise, more water, m re air pollution, more light pollution, more consumpt lestruction; and just as new roads lead to more cars, to yet more roads, so new development means more ss social stability, which leads to calls for more develop h leads to more mobility etc. It is a self-destructive cy can never be satisfied.

But where are the resources for this development? Where is the water for the new development at Hemel Hempstead, Stevenage and even my own district of South Cambridgeshire? To develop in areas where water is already short is irresponsible – it is Third World in outlook and concept. So why is water not a planning issue? Scientists tell us that East Anglia and the South east are going to get drier; the water authorities are asking for consultation in major planning decisions, but their pleas are being ignored. For those who doubt the seriousness of the position, visit the River Gade near Hemel Hempstead, where 7000 more houses are to be built. It is close to where Mr Michael Meacher, the Environment Minister grew up as a boy. A few years ago when I saw it in mid-summer it was a famous trout river, with kingfishers and yellow iris; today, in mid-winter, 'February fill-dyke', it is dry through over abstraction. So where is the water for 7000 extra houses coming from? Are the authorities in Hertfordshire going to copy those from Essex, piping millions of gallons of water from Norfolk to Essex, when Norfolk is already one of the driest counties in the country?

In theory the Environment Agency is supposed to stop such environmental disasters: in practice the Environment Agency is a toothless watchdog with no bark, no bite and no vision; it simply watches its own back, to make sure that it does not upset the Government, its political paymaster.

The proposed new developments and regional and district quotas are unwanted excesses, designed only to stimulate short term economic activity. On environmental grounds they should be stopped. Was Mr Prescott serious in Japan or not?

It is time we set an example. Before Mr Prescott allows another bout of land grabbing, polluting, consuming development, he should contemplate three simple facts. In Britain there is one car for every three people – in India there is one car to every eight hundred people; in America there is enough waste metal buried every year to make two million cars. To allow the developing world to reach our economic level the atmosphere would have to be eight times its size for there to be no climate change. In other words, continuous development based solely on market forces, selfishness and political whims and social fancies equal future environmental disaster on a massive scale. Is this what the Millennium celebrations are all about – celebrating the birth of the Millennium that will see the end of the human species and society as we know them? Even lemmings are not that misguided. It is time for the madness to stop.

But if the environmental grounds for this proposed new building spree cannot be justified, what are the social arguments? Again, sadly, they are a spin of confused and phoney political hype and economic nonsense, with development and municipal greed being concealed as social need. The claim is that with more family breakdowns and more single households, a dramatic increase in housing units is required. The facts are that the population is almost static, (apart from an influx from Europe due to the E.U.'s open border policy), that most of those involved in marriage breakdowns usually begin other shared relationships and so the perceived problem is not there. It is true that over the past thirty years the average household size has declined from four to 2.5, but this is not a problem of acute housing need, it is an additional market created by affluence, for the young, free and single. As a Stevenage councillor said on television recently: 'Single people have a right to improve their lifestyles'. So, apparently it is a 'right' now to take thousands of acres of Green Belt, with no concerns for the environmental 'rights' of future generations.

In this context the whole concept of 'rights' is absurd; how can we have a right to good health, in a world where there is disease? A right to clean air, when our lifestyles pollute? A right to new, personal housing when we are already Europe's most densely populated and over-crowded country. Consequently we should not be talking about rights, but about responsibility, sustainability and accountability. Why cannot the young and affluent continue to share the family home, until they need their own family home – that is being really responsible and sustainable?

The problem is of course that politicians have created a society based on mobility, which works against the whole concept of family units and communities. Yet communities build continuity and stability; mobility leads to fragmentation and a lack of social cohesion – the very social problems that are currently almost out of control.

Planners and developers may claim that they are building for local housing needs, the truth is that most developments are now for a moving population. Mobility of labour has turned the middle classes into little more than sophisticated gypsies, with the pantechnicon replacing the gypsy caravan and Mr Barrett or Mr Wimpey providing the temporary roofed camp-sites.

In my own area it is said we must have another 71,000 houses in the latest Prescott land-grab, and the apologists claim that this speculative growth will provide housing and work for local people. The truth is that they will provide homes for incomers from all over Britain moving into the high-tech industries clustering around Cambridge. Already in the villages close to Cambridge it is possible to hear the accents of Scotland, Wales, and Yorkshire more readily than a genuine Cambridgeshire drawl. This means that we are repeating the same mistakes for the technological revolution as were made during the industrial revolution. In addition to high-tech immigrants, the invasion will include those who want to be within easy commuting distance of London and the South-East.

As they come into the Cambridgeshire countryside, many will bring urban values with them. They will want better street lights, tidy verges, the village green cut like a lawn and a conveniently placed superstore erected. They will complain about the rook droppings in the school playground, the crowing of cocks, the bleating of sheep, mud on the verge, the sound of the grain drier, and they will be outraged by the passing of the hunt three fields away. Building in the countryside means urban colonisation and the death of the countryside. In a nearby parish one farmer whose family has lived in the centre of the village since 1830 has just relocated his farmyard; he can stand the difficulties caused by the surrounding new houses no longer.

Of course many of the apologists for development directly benefit from it. If they have development land, they claim social need and praise the first-time buyer, but it is the executive house that seems to take priority and make the money. As a young district councillor, twenty-eight years ago, I was most impressed when I heard a councillor pleading for development to keep his village 'alive'. It was only later that I learned that he actually owned some of the development land, and not once did I hear him declare an interest. Almost in a similar vein, Lord Spencer's spokesman is claiming that the 400 acres of the Althorp Estate going for development will help the social needs of Northampton; it is a difficult concept for those living on or near the site to grasp. Evidently it is far easier for Lord Spencer to take this benevolent view as he sits in his living room 8000 miles away in South Africa.

Unfortunately the whole nonsense of development is unstoppable; the Government decides the numbers, the Counties select distribution and the Districts have to implement, even when there is no room left. The whole system favours development and has done so since Labour introduced the Town and Country Planning Act in 1947. As my local Planning Director says: 'There is a presumption in favour of development'.

I now serve on my local Planning Committee and see the

system in action; it is totally weighted against the wishes of local communities, objectors and sustainability and makes a mockery of the whole concept of local democracy. If a development application fails, then the developer can keep coming back, almost wearing the planning committee down. The developer can also be asked to negotiate an acceptable scheme with the planners – there is no opportunity for objectors to negotiate in order to foil a proposed development. If the developer still fails he can then appeal and some of the most ludicrous planning consents that I have known have been made by Planning Inspectors. Here again the system favours development; it costs money to put a coherent case at appeal. Large development companies know the ropes and can afford to fight; local objectors usually operate on a shoe-string.

But, we are told, there is still one more safeguard – the Ombudsman. I have experienced him, too. He is another watchdog with no teeth, and in my experience without much interest either. In the early nineties we were told in South Cambridgeshire that we would have to house a large development. Many of us objected and were instructed by the then Chief Executive that if we continued to object, we would be surcharged – unsurprisingly the principle for a development went through.

The local MP (now retired) Sir Anthony Grant, established that the whole idea of surcharging was incorrect. Consequently when the choice of a development site for the 3000 houses came to be discussed, a number of us again made it clear that we would object to all development. At the start of the decision-making meeting the Council Chamber was cleared of public and press and councillors were told by the Planning Legal Officer that if they still objected, the developers would be able to claim up to £1m from the council in costs and compensation; unsurprisingly, development was passed by one vote. Again, later, it was suggested that this advice was unsoundly based, and many councillors still do not understand the reason for it. Consequently a local parish council chairman took the case to the Ombudsman, having craftily left a tape recorder recording during the confidential part of the meeting. For his trouble the objector was reprimanded by the Ombudsman for recording a private meeting and no action was taken. The validity of the information given by the Legal Planning Officer was apparently of no concern.

I then took the case up with the Ombudsman; peculiarly I had to do it as a private individual, not as a councillor, and I included in my evidence several examples of the council not following its own rules and ignoring the Government's own Planning Policy Guidelines; I know, I was there at all the meetings concerned. The case was clear cut; needless to say I lost and the Ombudsman was dismissive. I should not have been surprised; a former senior planning officer in East Anglia who has seen the system from the inside, now in private practice, says: 'All you get from the Ombudsman is a mixture of whitewash and soft soap. On virtually all important matters the Ombudsman sides with the planning authority regardless – the relationship between planning departments and the Ombudsman is far too cosy; it's all Christian name terms of course – the complainant is always assumed to be wrong'.

But the system gets even worse. Now, thanks to the Tories, built into major planning applications are offers from developers to improve local amenities or even the local infrastructure. Consequently a form of legalised bribery has actually been built into the system. The scale and type of development can take second place to what the developer is offering to give back.

And what about the opportunities for fraud and abuse? Here the British system of libel prevents an open discussion on the probable abuses of the planning system, just as it managed to protect Robert Maxwell for many years. All I can say is that I have seen many councillors at parish, district and county level benefit from the system and the police show little interest in claims of abuse. Incredibly too, totally bogus information can be given in planning applications, in an effort to change the value of land from 'agricultural' to 'development', and apparently such creative applications break no laws whatsoever.

With such a flawed, potentially corrupt and undemocratic system, a further 4.4 million houses in Britain pose a major threat to the British countryside and country people. Consequently I really am proud to be a NIMBY and I hope that other country dwellers are proud to be NIMBIES too. Tomorrow I shall be joining thousands (possibly hundreds of thousands) of people in London for the Countryside March. We shall be marching not simply about development, but about all the other assaults currently being levelled against the countryside – the ludicrous ban on T-bone steak, the closure of village schools and shops, the elimination of our hill farms and family farms, the pollution by poison, light and noise, the theft of our land and water, the parliamentary assault on our country sports, etc, etc. I will be marching with butchers and bakers, farmers and shepherds, huntsmen and housewives, NIMBIES, NOTES and BANANAS. It will be the largest, the politest and the most important protest London has ever known. It will be the countryside fighting back – not against Cool Britannia, but against the whole political establishment – Fool Britannia.

30

The House of Commons Funny Farm

————

The meat madness continues to spread apace, mainly affecting the politicians who want to ban it. And to think that poor old Douglas Hoggwash took the blame; now, Dr Jack Low-Cunningham is showing that he can be just as gullible and inept. There is even talk of banning bone in lamb, with the politicians, scientists and bureaucrats giving no evidence whatsoever for their fears. Presumably they have discovered that if a sheep has massive doses of BSE injected into its brain it contracts BSE – oh, what a surprise. No doubt if the same sheep had vast quantities of gin and tonic from a House of Commons bar injected into its head, it would behave just like some MPs.

I heard a very interesting and accurate joke the other day. What is the difference between a supermarket trolley and an MP? The supermarket trolley has a mind of its own and an MP is always getting filled up with food and drink.

I feel so sorry for small livestock farmers that as I was in the Black Hole when the Welsh farmers lobbied Parliament I went along to give moral support. As I approached wearing my winter beard and woolly hat I was instantly recognised, 'Look Dai' one said to his friend, 'here comes Bill Oddie'.

The most interesting aspect of the lobby of Welsh farmers was the fact they were all obviously working farmers. Just the colour of their cheeks and the way they walked proved that they were hard-working, 'hands-on' farmers. A visit to the recent Oxford Farming Conference was just as enlightening. It was immediately clear to me that a large majority of those attending the most influential farming conference in Britain were distinctly 'hands-off' farmers; in fact most of them were not even farmers, but the assorted parasites of the agri-farming industry – bankers, consultants, accountants, etc. Most of these gentlemen would have regarded the Welsh farmers as 'inefficient', 'uncompetitive', etc, etc. It is strange how the last person who actually has any say in farming policy these days seems to be the working farmer.

For me one of the most interesting aspects of the Conference was being at Oxford itself. Coming from near Cambridge I had always tried to avoid Oxford as being inferior, but was quite pleasantly surprised. One field in which Oxford excels is homelessness; it has even more beggars than Cambridge, a feat that I would have thought impossible in New Britain under New Labour. A sprinkling of dossers obviously had drink and mental problems, but many seemed to be members of the hobby-homeless; young, able-bodied, with a dog to attract money and sympathy – no doubt most of them will end up as social workers.

The first speaker at the Conference was billed as Dr Jack Cunningham, Secretary of State for Agriculture. I believe it was a glove puppet with the hand of the EU Agricultural Commissioner Frans Fischler up its back. Everything said seemed to be in praise of the EU and CAP Reform. Unfortunately everybody knows that CAP reform will not take place and the bland Tony Blair has dropped it from his immediate European agenda.

The first question was also a surprise; it came from somebody looking remarkably like the NFU's President, Sir David Naish, although he was not listed as a delegate. Consequently I think it was another glove puppet, this time with Jack Low-Cunningham's hand up its back. I wonder if Sir David Naish follows the Secretary of State everywhere; if he does then it must resemble a sort of Pinky and Perky Agricultural Road Show. I am looking forward to the day when the President of the NFU does not receive a knighthood while in office. To me that will illustrate that he or she has fought for ordinary farmers, and not simply buttered up to the farming and political establishments.

Not only were Dr Low-Cunningham and Mr Fischler present, but the American Secretary for Agriculture, Senator Dan Glickman, was also there. It was easy to see why the Americans do so well in negotiations; Senator Glickman was obviously Premier League quality; Dr Cunningham was Division Two, whereas poor old Frans Fischler was more like Division Six South of the Shepton Mallet Clodhoppers League. Amazingly, during the course of his address Frans Fischler described himself as a 'politician'; funny, I thought politicians had to be elected whereas European Commissioners were unelected, unaccountable and uncontrollable.

I asked Mr Fischler a very difficult question, 'As more people have died from eating peanuts than beef in the last twelve months, are you going to ban the sale of peanuts throughout Europe?'. It must have been difficult because he could not answer it.

Several of the few working farmers present complained to me that 'One Man and His Dog' is being shown at a most ridiculous time this year – 4.30 on BBC 2, Saturday afternoons. I agreed with them, it is a mad time – those farmers with sheep will be checking their sheep, while those farmers without sheep will be listening to the football results. Someone came up to me the other day and said, 'I saw you on television the other day'. He must have got it wrong; I did 'One Man and His Dog' without a beard. I expect I had been mistaken for Bill Oddie again.

31

The Lark Ascending

———

The short and hectic history of the Countryside Restoration Trust has taken another exciting and unexpected turn – we have been successful in our Heritage Lottery Fund bid and soon 140 acres of almost wall to wall wheat will be ours, turning our experimental plot of about one hundred acres into a farm of 240 acres. Because the new land is so featureless – a tribute to modern, industrialised farming – it will become our much wanted 'Lark Rise Farm'. In addition, as it arrived so soon after the launch of our 'Sir Laurens van der Post Memorial Appeal', it will be called the Sir Laurens van der Post Lark Rise Farm.

The land will form part of a fitting tribute to Sir Laurens, our first Patron, and it is an honour that HRH The Prince of Wales has become Patron of the two-year-long Appeal. The CRT was part of Sir Laurens' vision – how had farming become detached from nature? How had agriculture lost its 'culture'? How had people managed to sever their links with both nature and the land? And could the ruined land of modern food production be restored? The CRT was established as an attempt to provide some of the practical solutions to these questions, and the purchase of this new land will help us to provide a showcase for our brand of sympathetic yet productive farming. Although on a comparatively small scale at the moment, the principles involved apply to all land and people wherever they are. Indeed at a time when the 'global market' is in danger of turning all productive land into a food production line, while simultaneously driving people off the land in unprecedented numbers – threatening to destabilise the rural populations of developed and developing countries alike – the aims of the CRT are becoming more relevant every day.

The arrival of the new land for sale was totally unexpected. It came at a time when the CRT had seen the need to look for new land for the Laurens van der Post Memorial Appeal; astonishingly when it came on the market the block of 140 acres was situated right next to the land the CRT already owned. Laurens would have regarded this remarkable coincidence as 'synchronicity'. For anybody who doubts the astonishing nature of this sale, the land was in two blocks. Forty acres which had been owned by St Catherine's College, Cambridge for several hundred years, and the adjoining one hundred acres that had been owned by Corpus Christi College since 1342 – so the sale could hardly be regarded as short term property speculation.

The land had been originally acquired by Corpus Christi through the patronage of Henry Duke of Lancaster, whose subtenant had been one Sir Bartholomew Burwash (Burghersshe), a career soldier serving under the Duke during the Hundred Years War. The large field, lying in the valley of the Bourn Brook, close to Byron's Pool, where the brook flows into the Cam, lies between the villages of Barton and Grantchester. It was enclosed from open strip cultivation in 1839 and various parts of it had names to suit the age – 'Nine Stitches', 'Nine Stitches Furlong', 'Point Riddy Furlong', and where the ploughing was East/West instead of North/South – 'Cross Furlong'.

What makes the land even more interesting is that several local men know it well and remember the hedgerows and field patterns before it became 'prairiefield'. They recall the wildlife too, the lapwings, the cowslips, the skylarks and even snipe 'drumming'. As one says: 'At every corner there was something to see and something happening'. In the intervening years it has been turned into an almost featureless block of cereal production. Our aim will be to continue farming while bringing it back to life. In just five years we will want visitors to say again: 'At every corner there was something to see and something happening'.

Both the bid and the sale were nerve racking. The land was for sale on the open market, although the colleges did allow the last bids to arrive on the day after the vital meeting of the Heritage Lottery Fund Trustees. A small group of us burnt the mid-night oil preparing the bid – as I was fighting the Winchester By-Election at the same time it was more like burning the pre-dawn oil. John Terry the local FWAG officer, Margaret Taylor, the Trust Administrator, Tim Scott, our tenant farmer, Andrew Edwards, a Trustee and Gordon Beningfield, my vice-chairman – a constant support and inspiration – put together the application, including a business plan written in just 36 hours. We lost another piece of land that came on the market from a local farmer in mysterious circumstances and as time passed I became increasingly pessimistic. Several large landowners are still awash with money due to the present subsidy system and as our bid had to be within 10% of the District Valuer's valuation I thought we were doomed. One of my worries was how to pick the Trust up and regain momentum after failure?

Then we heard that we would be granted £372,000 towards purchase and restoration, if the colleges accepted our bid. It took the colleges a further week to come to their decision. I was elated but totally exhausted, and looked for the catch – there wasn't one – we had the money and the land would be ours; it was a tremendous honour. The worth of our philosophy had been recognised by experts in high places and the work and loyalty of our volunteers and 'Friends' had been rewarded. It meant that in just 4 $\frac{1}{2}$ years the CRT had grown from no land, no money and no members to a charity with nearly 4,500 'Friends' and 240 acres of land, and it had raised nearly £1m.

Until harvest the new land will be farmed extremely intensively, as it is already sown, but as soon as the combine leaves the last field things will change. The flood plain of the Bourn Brook will be put back to grass, which will give us nearly two miles of brook bank and traditional grass meadows. We then hope to join the Government's new and exciting Arable Stewardship Scheme – a pilot scheme being run in two areas of England and we are fortunate to be in one of them. It will enable us to divide the prairie into smaller fields, planting hedges, creating beetle banks, sowing grass margins and leaving cultivated margins just to see what seeds if any remain in the soil. We will be able to leave winter stubble and sow spring cereals, with every conservation friendly feature attracting an annual payment. We are already monitoring the land, so that as soon s the husbandry changes we hope to see wildlife beginning to come back. We hope too, that if the wildlife return is similar to that on the land already owned by the CRT, then the Government, and the European Commissioners, can be persuaded to divert CAP subsidies towards environmentally friendly farming, instead of industrial farming.

To help us in this task we would like to make a television documentary to show how quickly land can be restored – from lifeless prairies to living fields. Sadly such a film would take about five years to make, and both the BBC and the Independent Television Companies no longer seem interested in long term projects.

This exciting development in the life and times of the CRT does not represent the end of our aims, but a springboard for new projects. In the short term we would like to achieve 500 new members so that we can reach 5000 by the time of our fifth anniversary in July. By the end of December 1999 and the close of our Sir Laurens van der Post Memorial Appeal we would like to have purchased another property, preferably in the West country. In the long term we hope for a series of demonstration farms throughout the country, covering a variety of soils, conditions and traditions, including an upland farm and an organic farm. We hope to purchase land and we are willing to receive gifts of land, giving a guarantee of sympathetic, wildlife friendly farming.

With the progress made since our launch, the skylark of the CRT's logo has fluttered from the ground. With so much still to do it is vital that we keep the lark ascending.

32

North-West Passage

Until recently I had never been to the very North West corner of Scotland, although I had wanted to go for years. Then, out of the blue came a telephone call from the very North West tip of Scotland, would I go and speak to the Eddrachillis and Durness Branch of the Scottish Crofters Union? It was an interesting proposition – an English peasant talking to Scottish crofters; what would we have in common?

Evidently I have much in common with the traditional high-lander, as my first reaction was 'No, it will cost too much money'. But then the telephoning crofter assured me that although the Scottish Crofters Union was not a rich organisation, they would make a contribution towards expenses – so the trip was on.

I love Scotland, and somewhere in my ancestry a dose of Scottish blood crept in. Once in Scotland I stopped off at Reindeer House in the Cairngorms, to see my old friends Alan and Tilly Smith. They were enjoying a winter with almost no snow; for them it meant that bored non-skiers were flocking to see the reindeer. As a result their harvest had come early.

It is a beautiful area, now threatened with a funicular railway. Astonishingly this white elephant and environmental disaster is being backed by both Scottish Heritage and the EU. Time and time again I am told how the EU is our environmental hope for the future – it is a pity nobody seems to have told the EU.

Not only do Alan and Tilly Smith have reindeer, they now also have a herd of fallow deer and a flock of Sohay sheep. The sohays, out on wild pasture, make wonderful lamb, with mint sauce or red currant jelly. However, their new venture is threatened. If a lamb on the bone ban comes in for all sheep over a year old, as threatened by the absurd Dr Cunningham and Mr Rooker, then sohay chops will disappear – sohays are usually sold at eighteen months.

While we were watching the sheep a male hen harrier began to quarter old bracken across the valley. It was a wonderful sight – they seem to float just above the ground, sometimes stopping, but never apparently stalling. The harrier is one of my favourite birds of prey to watch; with their aerial expertise it is hardly surprising that they are so efficient at dining well on ground nesting birds.

To me there is no 'hen harrier problem'. If each estate could guarantee just one pair of breeding harriers each year; there would then be hen harriers, and the red grouse, golden plovers, dunlin, lapwing, curlews, etc would be able to survive as well. It is sad that conservationists will not be honest or practical about the problems caused by too many predators on bird populations. Recently 'BTO News', the newsletter of the British Trust for Ornithology, an organisation I usually admire, carried the headline, 'Moorland raptors reveal complex associations with prey'. The relationship between the hen harrier and prey is not complex at all; one is eaten by the other and when harrier numbers are high they have the same effect on moorland birds as my Hoover on dirt on the living room carpet.

The crofters were a jolly bunch and the scenery and coastline were spectacular. The men and women were following that old Scottish tradition of downing whisky and beer at the same time – I was glad it was Lent and I had given up spirits, otherwise any effort to keep up with them would have put me under the table.

The first question was surprising – not about the various threats to all of us on the land, but why had BBC's 'One Man and His Dog' been shown at 4.30 on Saturday afternoons, when all those present had been out checking their own sheep? The answer was easy; the BBC simply is quite clueless about the wishes and way of life of its rural audience, so it would have been more surprising if the series had been scheduled for a time when crofters, peasants and shepherds could watch it.

It was a tremendous meeting, and yes that old Scottish trait finally reared its amusing head again. One crofter, representing several of his friends had recently sold some sheep to a dealer from Cumbria. 'Do you know what he wanted' the seller said in tones of utter amazement, 'he wanted luck money – he wanted me to give him some money back, for buying my sheep'. I explained that in many parts of England this still was a tradition – in horse sales as well, and it was quite common to give £5, £10 or even £20 back to the buyer for 'good luck'. The crofter was not impressed: 'I didn't pay it,' he said, 'I told him I could pay nothing without holding a committee meeting.'

So I headed for home. What a spectacular journey, past a little village with every building, including the telephone box, painted black and white, and the great long lochs of More, Merkland and Shin. At one place I halted to watch a red-throated diver battling against the wind-whipped waves. These are hills with wildlife and people still working the land – I hope Mr Cunningham's insensitive and ignorant 'restructuring' does not drive the crofters and the estate owners off the land. Then I remembered something – yes, it had happened again – my pockets were empty – the crofters had 'forgotten' that simple word 'expenses' – perhaps they hadn't held a committee meeting.

33

Of Mice And Men

Over recent years part of my hovel has been trying to fall down. The reason is said to be 'drought' and not the heavy lorries that appear to shake the foundations of my house as they pass. On one occasion the Fantasy Department of Cambridgeshire County Council informed me that the house was too far from the road to pick up lorry tremors; presumably this impossible fact means that I tremble and shake every time a lorry passes and the house remains perfectly still. So, the cracks and yawning chasms have been caused by 'drought' – it's official.

At last builders have arrived and poured tons of concrete into the foundations to stop my bed being tipped into the adjacent ditch as I sleep. Now, by amazing coincidence, when the lorries pass I have stopped shaking and trembling, and the house seems totally stable as well.

The building work has had a dramatic effect on the local wildlife population, upsetting the winter routine of some of Britain's last remaining free-ranging wild mammals – mice. Normally my mice live quietly in the garage during the winter, eating, sleeping and breeding in piles of assorted junk. To allow the builders in, the garage had to be cleared, rendering all the poor little mice homeless. I hope the dreadful Michael Foster MP does not hear of this or we will be getting a Save Our Furry Friends Bill in Parliament, forbidding people to clean out their garages in winter. As a direct consequence of my actions, all the mice, and their friends, have now moved into my living room and kitchen.

There, they have warmth, comfort and a ready supply of food and they even come out to play when I have visitors. My first response to this invasion was to rouse Bramble into action. Sadly, at 15 $\frac{1}{2}$ the heart is willing, but the eyes rarely see mice, and the ears never hear them. I suspect that these outrageous mice even play on him when he sleeps – sliding down his rib cage and hiding in his long, warm coat.

Plan two was to trap them and out came the famous 'Little Nippers'; they were very effective, they caught my index finger, my thumb and the nose of a visiting Jack Russell terrier, but nothing else. They were either too lightly set and self destructed at the slightest vibration, or they became stuck, allowing the mice to not only eat the bait, but also perform gymnastics on the spring mechanism.

After much searching I managed to purchase two metal spring traps, and a 'humane' tunnel trap. The mice then proceeded to run along the top of the tunnel and they are turning their noses up at assorted baits of chocolate, cheese and new bread, that actually appeal to me.

Fortunately I am not the only one with a plague of mice. Two hundred yards up the road, old Bill has got them in his shed. He was alerted to the invasion on finding butterfly wings all over the floor – something was eating the hibernating butterflies and leaving the wings – rather like me with roast chicken. Mouse droppings betrayed the guilty parties and he was furious. Now he is getting his revenge on the butterfly murderers by using a very old method of mouse control – he is feeding them with plaster of Paris. He is hoping to find the bodies and exhibit them later on in the year at the National Gallery; I believe that with a small piece of imagination the Turner Prize could be his.

From time to time I get asked to speak at various functions about the farm, the CRT, how I came to write for *The Daily Telegraph*, etc. Sometimes I accept and sometimes I refuse; sometimes I ask for money and sometimes I do it for nothing, it all depends on the moon, mood and the state of my bank balance.

Recently an old friend, a Baptist minister, asked me to speak at a Baptist Men's Dinner. I must confess that at first glance this did not have a great deal of appeal, but then I remembered that Dronfield was close to an area that housed an interesting wild beast – the Beast of Bolsover – so I accepted. Now I will readily admit that I am not the snappiest dresser in the land – unlike my colleague Mr Poole, but at least I am comfortable. Contrary to local suggestion I do own a tie and use it regularly to keep my trousers up when I can't find my belt. But what clothes do you wear for a Baptist Men's Dinner – a dinner jacket, casual clothes, or sackcloth and ashes?

I decided to remain comfortable in newish jeans, sports shoes and open-necked shirt. On arrival at the manse I sensed I had made the wrong decision when my host asked: 'Would you like to change now?' As we arrived at the venue I could not believe my eyes, it was not a draughty church hall, but an exclusive local Golf Club – I was in big trouble. No sooner had I arrived, than a club official asked me to leave; the after dinner speaker was being ejected before dinner had even started – is this a record?

The Minister was traumatised; he had two options, he could accept fate, or perform a modern-day miracle; he chose the latter.

A high speed tour of Dronfield followed, begging and borrowing second-hand clothing. We obtained trousers that were too long and shoes that were too big, but at least they prevented the trouser legs from dragging on the ground; then with a tie and jacket that would not do up we arrived again, just before the soup. As I walked in I felt like Charlie Chaplin without his cane.

It ended up being a very entertaining evening and I learnt an important fact; apparently I can avoid any future sartorial humiliation by purchasing something called 'a suit'. If a suit can be worn with wellington boots and a woolly hat, then I think I will get one.

34

Fantasy Land

With the whole world being hyped up by the media to think only in terms of football and football analogies I am pleased to have witnessed over recent weeks a terrific hat-trick, scored by the Environment Agency; it is just a pity that they have all been own goals.

The most spectacular were the floods around the Ouse and the Nene – pronounced so beautifully by the BBC as 'Nen'. For over twenty-five years I have been trying to point out that if all our ditches, brooks, streams and rivers are dug out to act like fast-response drains the result is disaster; when it rains our river systems are turned into giant cisterns, flushing the water away in record time. The fact that in Eastern England this water is needed to recharge acquifers seems irrelevant to the EA – they just want to get this valuable natural resource into the North Sea as soon as possible.

This 'improvement' then allows the natural 'flood plains' to be cultivated, because they rarely flood. The fact that when the water rushes from the land its flow now washes nitrates and chemical sprays into the river systems seems unimportant. The recent flood came at a time when the crops had just been sprayed and fertilised so the flood water became a chemical cocktail.

Because many of the flood plains are attractive, close to water, and usually dry, greedy developers, environmentally illiterate planners and councillors, and gullible buyers, then build on them – yes, they build on areas that traditionally flood and then show great surprise when they do flood. Sometimes the flood plains are raised to make the buildings safe; because the rivers are then unable to use them, the water backs-up and floods areas up stream, as appears to have happened at Bedford.

Finally the drainage engineers defend their madness; Mr Jobsworth says: 'To prevent flooding we must do more dredging and draining at more regular intervals'. This achieved, next time there is unusually heavy rain the floods are even more spectacular and the insurance claims higher.

The solution is easy; rivers should be allowed to flood on their flood plains, to slow the flow – it is as simple as that. Fortunately I am not the only one to have come to these conclusions. The RSPB and the Wildfowl and Wetlands Trust seem to agree, after witnessing years of high speed flash floods wiping out the nests of rare breeding birds at the Ouse Washes. Unfortunately if a more natural system was allowed, Mr Jobsworth and his friends would become unemployed, and of course it is Mr Jobsworth who advises our environmentally illiterate politicians on flooding.

Interestingly the floods came just after the BBC had flaunted its 'Water Week' – one of many patronising and superficial looks at the countryside following the success of the Countryside March. However, after wallowing in water for a week, the floods caught Auntie by surprise and no sensible or informed analysis appeared. Indeed, in the weekend of the floods, that marooned flagship, Countryfile, the urban journalist's view of the country-side, had as its main topic anti-biotics in animals; a subject dealt with by most informed commentators years ago.

The EA's second own goal involved the giant chemical company Agrevo, at their factory near Cambridge. For years there have been fears concerning land near this plant as it appears to be polluted. During this time the statutory authorities responsible for dealing with pollution seem to have been falling over themselves to take no action. Even the new Under Secretary of State for the Environment, Angela Eagle, has been sucked into the system of doing nothing.

Last April I was called to a small brook near the factory. A liquid was gushing into the brook from the factory (it was a time of drought when all the other ditches and streams into the brook had dried up and a year after the gushing drain was supposed to have been decommissioned). I could smell the chemical cocktail thirty yards away, so I phoned the EA. Incredibly I was told that nobody was available to visit. The local Chief Environmental Health Officer then phoned to say they had to visit as it was their statutory duty.

When I eventually heard that Agrevo was going to be prosecuted I phoned the EA wanting to be a witness. The EA's solicitors had no record of my involvement or that of the Chief Environmental Health Officer. I was not called as a witness and Agrevo was fined the paltry sum of £2000. According to reports it was said that pollution 'seeped' into the brook, not gushed, and the fine was only double that of a dog fouling the grass verge in South Cambridgeshire. To us locals it seems that the Environment Agency is terrified of tangling with large powerful chemical companies.

The final own goal came when our local cement works was recently allowed to burn even more toxic waste; the percentage has gone up from 25% to 40%. As part of its consultation process the EA decided to hold a public meeting – without telling the public. A tiny advert appeared in a local paper and nothing more. Parish councils were not told and notices were not put up in the villages concerned. Fortunately others made up for the EA's lack of effort and the meeting was packed. The EA seemed unable to answer even the most basic questions and were mesmerised by the cement work's spokesman – Mr Clack. Quite unsurprisingly permission has now been granted. Some good did come out of the farce however; the cement company has promoted Mr Clack and he has moved away from the smoking chimney.

35

Artificial Cats and Swinging Bats

—

I am just surfacing from a triple deluge of letters on planners, bird tables and mice. I will try to answer every one, but if I do it will be a miracle. My thanks in particular to all those who wrote and phoned with foolproof advice about getting rid of mice. They all had one thing in common – they didn't work. My mice are still rampant and I am almost at my wits' end; Bramble however remains totally relaxed. At almost sixteen he can still catch, with remarkable agility, a Bonio skimming across the carpet – but mice that change direction? He has lost interest.

Among the baits that readers have recommended with absolutely no effect were Hobnob biscuits, dry bread, Red Leicester cheese, Stilton, peanuts, peanut butter, apple, chocolate, sultanas soaked in whisky and glacé cherries. With such a menu available the mice continue to ignore all six traps, and the so-called 'humane' tunnel trap is just a joke. Of course I can well understand why any self respecting mouse will not eat peanuts, or disgusting peanut butter, but even I had a nibble at the mature Stilton and the sultanas in whisky not only ruined my diet but also my Lent abstinence.

So how does the word get around in mouse society that traps are to be avoided – is it language, intelligence or what? I have even taken to reading all the available mouse literature to find out, from the charming world of the Brambly Hedge mice, to the informative and entertaining 'Mice and Voles' (Whittet Books) by

John Flowerdew, probably Britain's greatest mouse expert, but still the traps are empty, while my cupboards remain full.

Fortunately not all mouse invasions are bad. The other day the CRT had a maintenance day, with volunteers checking tree guards etc on all the hundreds of trees planted over the last four years. The small spinney has grown into a fascinating area. When we designed the spinney we decided to follow the pattern first made popular by God. In other words we planted the trees almost randomly – not in boring straight lines which seems to be the plan of MAFF, local authorities, agricultural colleges etc. After walking through woods designed by both God and MAFF we decided that God seemed far more sensible and imaginative.

God's plan also has one other great advantage, if the trees are not planted in straight lines, it means that the 'weeds' between them cannot be mown at regular intervals throughout the summer. Consequently in our spinney the 'weeds' provide wonderful cover and food for birds in winter, and in the summer the flowers and insects attracted provide yet more food as well as tangles of cover, ideal for nesting yellowhammers and English partridges.

By doing this we thought we were helping mainly birds and insects, but then, in a tree-tube one of our volunteers from Hertfordshire discovered something else. A beautifully woven nest of grasses, left over from the summer – it was the nest of a harvest mouse. During the course of the day we found several more, including another in a tree-tube. So God's spinney design had an unexpected bonus; it showed us that we have a good population of these wonderful little mice. Like so many farmland creatures harvest mice have suffered enormously from the intensification of farming; our area of weeds has shown that with the right habitat they will come back. The trees are growing well in their unregimented state and as they grow and the weeds are shaded out, we will make sure that a fringe of rough vegetation is left for this welcome little mammal. It is yet one more example of how quick and easy it is to get farmland creatures back, although admittedly the return of the harvest mouse has been a complete accident, albeit a very welcome one.

Of course some trees probably should be planted in straight lines, particularly if they are regarded as a 'crop'. We are considering one of these on a small piece of low lying land. It is a magnificent tree and one of the few to have changed the course of history – the cricket bat willow.

To study the social and economic aspects of the cricket bat willow, I recently made a trip of great hardship and inconvenience to Barbados, to see how the wood stands up to overseas conditions. It did not take long to realise that if you are an English cricketer the willow stands up to the Caribbean very badly, but if you happen to be West Indian then it works amazingly well. Consequently I think we will plant willows for use by West Indians and I hope I live long enough to see a ball pinging to the boundary off a CRT bat. Despite obviously being work, it was a very enjoyable trip, organised by the old English fast bowler John Snow. In fact it was so good I now feel compelled to go to Australia next winter to see how the English willow performs over there.

I did all the things a modern, sophisticated English cricket-watcher does when he or she goes abroad. I bought a Barmy Army polo shirt, limbo danced under the seats during the rain breaks and listened to the Barmy Army choir with amazement. It should surprise no one that many of Britain's barmiest army appear to be solicitors, accountants, financial consultants and stockbrokers; in other words professional men behaving badly. My greatest achievement of all was to miss the wicket of Mark Ramprakash after his century, as I was preparing myself for the approaching Mexican wave. At least I saw more than one Yorkshireman; he seemed to spend the whole time watching the Test Match Special Commentary Box, to see who was commentating. Surely he would have found out far more cheaply by listening at home.

36

Sheep, Dogs and Ducks

———

For the second year running I have almost the latest lambing season in Britain. At a time when some people are already thinking of mint sauce, my little band of ewes are busily delivering their twins; by some strange quirk even the Suffolk lambs have come out black this year. My problem is that just when the ram should be at his busiest, I am also at mine – in a completely different sphere of activity I hasten to add. Tupping time is the time that I usually put aside for talking to assorted groups, and many days are spent travelling to farmers' clubs, hunt suppers and W.I.s. Consequently the tup has to go in with his ladies when I can find the time.

This year a neighbour put his in for me. I was astonished; it looked almost like a large lamb, hardly a ram, and much smaller than the ewes. I wondered whether I should get him a box to stand on. What is more he seemed far more interested in food than anything else and I never once saw him perform his duty. To add to the problem my neighbour had released him raddleless and so there was no way to measure his ardour.

By the time I took him out there were still no signs of love and passion and I assumed he was too small. At that time I dare not trying anything bigger, as I did not really want to lamb in June. I was resigned to having a lambless year, which did not really worry me as some of my ewes are rather on the geriatric side. I need not have worried; the lambs have arrived and they are a good strong bunch. How the miracle was achieved I will never know; I can only assume that the little tup really was a woolly jumper.

One problem over recent years has been the short supply of

grass due to drought. This year the problem is the exact opposite – too much grass. With the warm wet weather the grass has grown high, thick and lush. One little meadow is out of the question for lamb grazing, the grass is so high that they would get lost. I will put them instead in a beautiful small meadow that has already been partly grazed. The meadow is in the Countryside Stewardship Scheme, designed to encourage environmentally friendly farming and a degree of public access.

It seems to me that the Countryside Stewardship could be one of the answers to over-intensive farming, and it could also help close the town/country divide by getting people into the countryside where they can see farmlife at first hand. Sadly this does not take into account some of the bureaucrats who run the scheme. The meadow where my ewes were enjoying their pregnancies was in the Stewardship Scheme. To keep the old girls in and dogs out I used three low strands of electric fence and two tied hurdles. Incredibly this was not good enough for the MAFF administrator; the fence and the hurdles constituted a prevention of access – although various people climb the hurdles easily, and even I, not the tallest person ever created, can swing my legs over the wires without touching them. Apparently the hurdles must be untied, or even taken away; the MAFF man did not say whether he would round up the sheep if they get out and he was evidently unaware that dogs are not welcome amongst pregnant ewes or lambs. Public access is fine, but 'doggy' access is ridiculous. MAFF really must make up its mind whether it wants a living, working countryside, or an emasculated amenity and theme park.

I do like dogs and have never been without one, but the dog and cat issues in rural areas seem to be almost out of hand. There are simply too many of them. The cat is undoubtedly up there with the magpie and sparrowhawk as a major killer of songbirds and their young, and dogs are turning vast areas of the countryside into doggy latrines. On the farm we have a block of thirty acres of Stewardship Scheme grassland which I hoped would increase our lark population. With the sun shining and the larks singing it can provide people with a pleasant walk and a feeling of deep country. Sadly those occasions are few and far between

112

as usually there are people taking dogs for a 'walk'. Walk is not the right word; the dogs are usually off their leads, running, hunting and abluting at a time when nesting birds and breeding hares need peace and quiet.

Oh dear, my cricketing career and my creaking bones are now destined to continue until the end of 1999. My rule is that I retire in the season that I do not hit a six or score a fifty. Last year I left it to the last game of the season. This year I achieved both in the first game of the season. I attribute my success to my new trousers. Last year every vigorous shot led to the buttons bursting around my expanding middle. Consequently each hook shot carried the threat of me losing my trousers. Now with an elasticated middle, two inches larger than last year I can bat quite fearlessly while retaining my modesty and my dignity.

during our stint in the field I heard one of the most astonishing calls I have ever heard in years of playing cricket. One of the opposition batsmen dollied the ball up exactly half way between me and cover point. Both of us were on the point of charging for it; a collision looked likely. Our skipper then shouted something most helpful: 'One of you'. Consequently I left it for cover and cover left it for me; it was one of the greatest pieces of leadership I have ever experienced.

One of the few joys of fielding is being sent to long-leg where I like to watch the swallows feeding, high or low. Sadly, last Saturday there was not one swallow to be seen. I have never known a summer with so few swallows and I have only heard the cuckoo once.

One solitary swallow arrived at the barn in the farmyard where once four pairs nested. It only stayed two days and then it was gone. A few days earlier I had visited the Lake District and the swallow population seemed to be as healthy as ever. Consequently it seems to me that the swallow decline in East Anglia must be caused by the farming methods; the use of insecticides over thousands of acres of arable land, plus farmyards that are much too clean and tidy with no puddles and no doors left open so that swallows can nest.

Not all is bad bird news however, as this year the songs of the blackcap and the whitethroat seem to come from every thicket. Two days ago I also had a remarkable sight in my garden. A jay swinging violently on my peanut holder while stuffing itself with nuts. It was obviously a junk food jay.

37

A Good Man

———

I will always remember May 4th 1998. It was the day after my birthday; the sun was warm bringing out the first orange tip butterfly of the year and the apple blossom in my garden was at its peak. On the CRT land a thousand cowslips bloomed, and above, larks sang. There was a fusion of scents, sound and visual beauty; it was the art of nature. Such a day required a painting; a painting of a day that was quintessentially English. There was only one man who could have caught the mood to perfection – but tragically that was the day my friend Gordon Beningfield died.

There is always sadness after an illness bravely fought, but with Gordon the sense of loss has been intensified by the season of his going. He loved the spring and only ten days before he had said from his hospital bed: 'This is my favourite season of the year – what a time to be in here.' The legacy of paintings he leaves behind shows his love of the English spring – bluebell woods with fallow deer, 'windflowers', butterflies and an appreciation that made him the most outstanding countryside painter of his generation.

How I will miss him; as a friend, a confidant, my hoped for Best Man and as Vice Chairman of the Countryside Restoration Trust. It was at this time of year that the phone calls would come thick and fast 'I've seen my first swallow - my first swift - my first

114

orange tip.' His enthusiasm never faded and each year there would be new finds, new experiences, visits to Hardy Country, rides on steam trains, visits to this field, that reserve and even journeys to Duxford to see his favourite man made bird, the Spitfire. There too in the background was always Betty, his childhood sweetheart turned wife – companion, friend and certainly the best country cook in Hertfordshire.

We were friends from the instant we met, well over twenty years ago. He came to interview me about my tame vixen for a television programme. We had much in common; we were both uneducated innocents in a very competitive and predominantly urban world – he in painting and me with the pen. As time wore on our innocence showed still more; he produced illustrated books for what seemed an astonishingly small royalty, and I was writing for a publisher who sold his company and my royalties without telling me or the new owner.

Our interests were almost identical except for one thing – I was embarrassingly ignorant about butterflies. Gordon was a self-taught expert whose expertise showed itself in his paintings, as he transformed butterfly 'illustration' into genuine art. His enthusiasm pulled me into the world of butterflies: 'There's an orange-tip. Let's look for its eggs on the cuckoo flower,' and there they were.

His enthusiasm turned to anger as he saw the general countryside ruined by intensive farming and the CAP, thanks in his view to Edward Heath 'the traitor', or 'the bloater', according to his mood. Each ripped out hedgerow, ruined badger sett and felled tree he felt personally, a loss that depressed him and made him even more determined to fight the advance of the evil agricultural and planning empires. It was in 1980 that he decided we should enlist the help of the RSPB and we rushed off to Sandy to demand that the then Director, Ian Presst, make a stand for the general countryside and not just special reserves. Gordon banged the table in frustration to emphasise his point, something that does not happen to the head of the RSPB every day.

But although he felt the destruction of the countryside deeply, he could also be a very happy and funny man. Each year we would visit the Shire Horse Show at Peterborough and somehow he always got into the Press tent for a bacon sandwich breakfast. Then there was the Game Fair; he smart in his immaculate John Brocklehurst country clothes – the perfect gentleman; me in my trainers and jeans – the perfect peasant, and Badger Walker the eccentric rustic, making plastic bag caches at every antiquarian book stand.

I shared many public platforms with him over the years when he always spoke with passion, conviction and humour with not a note in sight. The halls were almost always packed for he had the common touch and people of all ages were attracted to him and loved him. In fact most, like me, could never understand why he ceased being on television, particularly when modern countryside programmes seem to be more an extension of the Telly Tubbies rather than an informed look at the countryside.

As we saw the countryside being steadily eroded the idea of the Countryside Restoration Trust gradually formed and he had no hesitation in becoming a Trustee – travelling to all the meetings, open days and the December barn dances.

When his illness returned it was hard. He desperately wanted to produce another book, Beningfield's Vanishing Song Birds and he completed some stunning new paintings. He hated missing the Countryside March; he did not hunt, he stopped shooting and his trout river dried up, but he believed that hunting, and all the other countryside issues of the CAP, the Green Belt, the closure of village schools, the power of the super-markets etc. were worth marching for.

Strangely, as I write this piece and another orange tip flutters through my garden I do not feel desolate. I feel honoured to have had such a friend and determined to continue the fight for the countryside he loved so much. Part of that determination, I hope, will lead to the CRT getting a farm in Dorset; his part of Hardy Country will become Beningfield Country. It will be a fitting tribute to an outstanding, good man.

38

Comings and Goings

Is it a record? I have just been to an agricultural show that actually still felt like an agricultural show, with not a teddy bear stall or double-glazing salesman in sight. Yes, the Suffolk Show is a real show, with real people, real farmers and real sheep and cows. I also met someone looking like a real politician; it was my old friend and adversary, on home ground, John Selwyn Gummer. Sadly, I can no longer call him John Seldom Glummer as I have never seen him looking happier: Opposition obviously suits him.

It is an amazing transformation. Even now as I look back on his time at MAFF and the Department of the Environment I surprise myself – his reign looks positively saintly compared with what followed. Douglas Hoggwash was bad enough, but the turmoil, gloom and doom that has descended on the farming community thanks to the political ineptitude of Dr Jack Low Cunningham makes the Gummer years seem like a sun-drenched paradise. I can hardly believe that I have written such words, but I have because they are true.

I was at the show for a very special reason. John Richards, one of the country's leading carriage drivers, had invited me to be a passenger – or ballast – on his carriage, drawn by four magnificent Gelderlanders. It is something I have always wanted to do and thoroughly enjoyed it, apart from one thing. For the first time in my life I had to wear a top hat. A top hat and trainers; the combination made me look like a debauched country squire; I'm relieved that appearances can be so deceptive.

Sheep dog trialling followed the carriages with the national

117

champions from all four home countries competing against one another in a close and entertaining competition. I wish the Controller of BBC 2 had been there. Not only was the crowd large and appreciative, but I was repeatedly stopped and asked: 'Why did they have "One Man and His Dog" on at 4.30 on a Saturday afternoon this year. I didn't see one as I was checking my animals. Are they trying to ruin the viewing figures so they can take it off? It's the only decent programme on the box these days.' I would have been interested to hear the all powerful Controller's reply. It was a superb, traditional little show; I will have to go again.

A few years ago the Suffolk Show experienced high drama. Sniffer dogs arrived to check the ground before the arrival of a member of the Royal Family. Suddenly a major alert was called and the main ring was cleared as the spaniels ran riot under the grandstand. Why had the IRA picked the Suffolk Show? The answer quickly came as a rabbit bolted for cover with the sniffer dogs sniffing in hot pursuit.

That is a story Gordon Beningfield would have liked. Looking back, that is what made him such good, happy company. Yes he did take the destruction of the countryside seriously, as he did his painting, but he also loved laughter.

His memorial service at St Albans Cathedral was a moving affair. It is a wonderful, ancient building and the scene seemed just right as 1000 people assembled to celebrate a remarkable life. It is strange how music can set off emotion; the service started with Vaughan Williams' 'The Lark Ascending'. I had never heard it played on the organ before; it was beautiful and the notes seemed to flutter down from the high vaulted roof. With the lark being the symbol of the CRT and of the English countryside in summer it took me many minutes to compose myself for my short address, one of four.

The end was as emotional as the beginning with 'Jerusalem' being followed by Holst's 'Jupiter'. I have never heard such inspired organ music. For years I have noticed the similarity between the atmosphere in a cathedral with the organ playing, and the mood found in an ancient wood with the birds singing.

If both have resulted from a random chemical cocktail oozing from the primeval slime then I will become a disciple of genetic engineering.

There is obviously an un-engineered humour gene in the Beningfield family tree, as prior to the service, Gordon's brother Roger sent me a simple mesasge. 'Don't forget to wash your trainers before you come.'

I did far better than that; I bought a pair of black leather shoes, the first all leather shoes I have worn for years. Now all I need is a suit to go with them – and yes, I have now ordered one of those, too.

The funniest incident involving Gordon occurred when we had gone to the Game Fair and were talking to some complete strangers. 'What do you do, mate?,' one of them asked him.

'I'm a painter,' Gordon replied.

'Really – could you give me an estimate for decorating my bathroom?'

Gordon somehow fought off laughter and simply said: 'Sorry, I don't do bathrooms.'

He loved laughter for laughter's sake. When he was unable to go on the Countryside March he wanted a full report. I told him of my highlight; travelling on the London underground with a carriage full of ordinary country people, many of whom had obviously seldom been to London before. At one station a group wanted to get out. 'How do you open the door?' they asked in a panic as they stretched high and low trying to find an exit. It was pandemonium until a kind person pointed to the button 'Push to Open'. Gordon laughed as much at the second hand story as I had in the carriage. Laughter and lark song are a good combination – they must both go on.

39

Nutty

———

As I sit here, perched up in the roof, writing this Diary, something special is happening; I have a woodpecker hanging from my nuts. It has never happened before, until this summer. I am not the only one of course, to have such pleasure; the other day I phoned the great and good Robin Hanbury Tenison to talk about palm nuts, one of the most environmentally unfriendly crops of tropical countries. I said to him: 'Guess what, I have a great-spotted woodpecker hanging from my nuts as we speak'; his reply was instant: 'What a coincidence: I've also got one pecking at mine.'

I get the two adults and a number of young and as they peck, blackbirds, robins and sparrows pick up the crumbs. At the moment my assorted gang of summer nut hangers are eating a whole peanut container every two days – a much faster rate than in the winter.

My summer feeding has been a great success with numerous adults and young of about ten species regularly arriving for a snack. One thing has puzzled me, after heavy rain blue tits and great tits seem to feed more often. With such behaviour it is handy having Nature Notes' Bob Burton living about eight miles away as the crow flies. He believes it is because the rain washes caterpillars, bugs, beetles and eggs from the leaves of trees and so there is less food available for the tits, consequently feeders are a handy backup for them.

The arrival of the woodpeckers has been a pleasant surprise. At one time I only saw great spotted woodpeckers occasionally in the winter. Now they are here the whole year long. Last week I had a green woodpecker on an ant hill at the bottom of what I call my 'garden' and two great spotted woodpeckers, one on the nuts and one having a drink.

The other morning I had a huge shock. Something large and white leapt onto the bird table and started tucking into stale bread. It was Hippy, the ever hungry Jack Russell of the CRT secretary who had arrived to invite me to visit the Royal Show with her.

Despite not needing any double-glazing or cuddly teddy bears, and despite my better judgement, I decided to go. It was an interesting journey, with me driving and she acting as navigator. Women are remarkable creatures, most seem to know the difference between right and wrong, but not right and left. Consequently Stoneleigh was reached following a wonderful journey along the byways and backroads of Northamptonshire and Warwickshire. It meant too that we went into the Royal Show along a windy back track with the trees on every bend being tied with red tape. I presume this was so that the Barley Barons from my neck of the woods could look up what they had seen in a "Prairie Farmers Guide to the Countryside': red tape = a tree. The tapes on the bends could also have had a subliminal message, that trees do not normally grow in straight lines.

After finding a car park as far away from the entrance as possible we put Hippy on a lead (amazing that some people think that I do not like dogs) and trekked past numerous officials to the main gate, only to be told firmly at the last possible moment 'no dogs'. Of course I could believe it, after all this was the Royal Show, with signs pointing to 'AgriBusiness'. At most genuine agricultural shows and country shows part of the enjoyment is to take your dog, and Bramble has visited many. The fact that the Royal Show denies entry to dogs, has no sheep dog trials or a gundog competition sums up the agribusiness and double-glazing domination of the show perfectly.

The reason for our visit was to watch the Inter-Hunt Team Relay, and the East Kent team in particular. It should surely be a demonstration sport at the next Olympics. I thought men and women on horses were supposed to jump over fences; several pink jacketed Masters had different ideas and seemed to specialise in going under and through the jumps, quite independently of their horses. It was very entertaining.

For me, the highlight of the Royal Show was the Farm Biodiversity Action Plan opened by the dreary Agricultural Minister Dr Jack Low Cunningham, at the Sainsbury's stand. The CRT talks to supermarkets regularly as we want to influence them and Sainsbury's is a corporate member. Indeed Sainsburys' environmental policy is about 'The Living Landscape', which they admit they lifted from CRT literature – which is fine, we are only too pleased to help. The aim of the Biodiversity Action Plan is to help landowners identify and help vulnerable species and habitats.

But why are Sainsbury's only trying to influence farmers – why don't they try to introduce the same standards to their own superstores? Recently Sainsbury's store in Cambridge had a swarm of bees at the rear of its premises, well away from customers and staff. Honey bees of course are 'a vulnerable species' at the moment, so what did Sainsbury's do? The Cambridge City dog warden was called for some reason, although even Sainsbury's should know that a bee is not a dog. The warden contacted Bill Clark, Head Warden of a nearby nature reserve. Being a bee keeper Bill Clark was keen to take the swarm and informed Sainsbury's that he would be about an hour. By the time he arrived, just after Rentokil, all that was left was a pile of dead bees with the odd scouts and foragers returning to drop dead on the poisoned swarm – so Sainsbury's 'living landscape' had become a dead heap and their action plan had been: 'Phone Rentokil'. It is surely time that the supermarkets decided whether their environmental concern is born out of conviction or soft-selling hype?

40

The Lark Song of Celebration

———

It seems impossible that it is already five years ago, almost to the day, that the Countryside Restoration Trust was launched on 15/7/1993. What a five years they have been; a roller coaster of highs and lows, achievements and failures, laughter and tears. From a position of no members, no money, no land and a group of trustees with no experience of running a charity, we have grown to expecting our 5000th member any day now, we have over 235 acres of land and we have raised nearly a million pounds.

I have been astounded by what has happened, at the support, the friendship and the enthusiasm of so many people. Reality contrasts so sharply with our original advice. 'Don't go public,' we were told by a financial consultant, 'your aims can't get public support and you will be lucky to raise £2000.' For that advice, of course, he wanted to charge over £2000. Bad advice is made to ignore; we ignored it and there has been no regret.

The gestation period of the CRT was a long one and the most influential figures during that time were Sir Laurens van der Post and Gordon Beningfield. Laurens provided a philosophical base tinged with sadness; as he saw agriculture being turned into an industrial process he was burdened by the way in which ordinary people were being cut off from nature and the seasons of the year. Gordon Beningfield on the other hand provided a mixture of both anger and enthusiasm. Anger at what he saw as the needless destruction of wildlife and landscape, and enthusiasm for the right to restore, conserve, attack (politicians) and convert the general public.

As we saw the growing crisis in the general countryside we

were frustrated by the political indifference and ineptitude. Indeed when I look back my concern dates back almost 25 years and my third book, *The Decline of an English Village* which was published way back in 1974.

In 1980 Gordon and myself took our worries for the general countryside to the RSPB, but reserves, SSSI's and 'island conservation' were the flavours of the time; hedgerows, wet meadows, declining farmland birds were off the agenda.

So the destruction, the industrialisation of farming went on and even accelerated under the influence of the Common Agricultural Policy – a policy driven by production, not the means of production, and a policy dominated by the words 'efficiency', 'productivity' and 'competitiveness', instead of 'quality', 'responsibility' and 'sustainability'.

By 1991 we had decided that the only thing to do was to start our own charity to change attitudes in farming, the general countryside and in conservation itself. We simply did not see the sense in having to make a car journey of twenty or thirty miles to see a barn owl or a bee orchid in a 'nature reserve', when they should have been living naturally in every rural parish. The idea was not to advise farmers how to farm, the Farming and Wildlife Advisory Group was already doing that, with mixed results; we decided to buy land turned into a wildlife desert by over-intensive farming and to 'show' how productive farming could be linked with attractive landscapes and abundant wildlife.

Laurens and Gordon immediately agreed to become Trustees, together with a few friends from a cross-section of backgrounds. But how do you launch a charity with a recession looming? That was the question. The answer came quickly and decisively. Forty acres of mono-culture became available alongside a small tributary of the Cam; we dithered, what should we do and how should we do it? Suddenly, out of the blue otters arrived in the small brook after thirty years of absence; our minds were made up. If we got the land we could turn the flood plain into wet meadows; the otter habitat would be improved and we could have arable where it was always meant to be, well away from the water.

On July 16th we launched the CRT; on July 24th I wrote about our launch in *The Daily Telegraph* and letters and money poured in. Hundreds of letters arrived, one containing a post card to which a pound coin was stuck with tape and another, from an ordinary countrywoman, contained a cheque for £10,000. That autumn we purchased the first twenty acres; in the spring we bought the remaining twenty acres and on our first anniversary we had just 800 members.

The original land has been transformed; wildlife has flooded back, our otters still visit regularly, and our tenant farmer has produced good crops. Now with generosity from my father and the Heritage Lottery Fund our length of brook has grown from 800 yards to two miles and our 235 acres represents a farm, 'Lark Rise Farm', and not an experimental plot. The skylark has become our logo, the symbol of a healthy countryside and this summer its song has been louder than for many years.

Our success has been mixed with bleak sadness. Elspeth Huxley, another founder trustee, died, as did Sir Laurens van der Post, who had become our first Patron. He would have seen our growth of land in one large block as 'synchronicity'. Then came the tragic loss of Gordon Beningfield still at the peak of his artistic creativity and brimming over with enthusiasm for the future.

We are determined to make the next five years as exciting as the last five and we are pleased that the RSPB and the Wildlife Trusts have also seen the growing crisis for farmland wildlife and farming communities in the general countryside. Our aim is to create a network of CRT owned farms throughout Britain covering different soils, farming traditions and cultures to spread the message. We want conservation, recreation, education and quality food production to take place on the same land. We also want to buy an orthodox farm and run it organically, as there are just as many challenges with organic farming as with conventional farming.

One thing too has caused us much anxiety over the last five years. Many times, at the death of an elderly, traditional farmer, with nobody to follow on, we have been contacted asking the

CRT to buy the farm to prevent it being bought and devastated by neighbouring intensive farmers. Sadly we are always told at the last minute and so have neither the time nor the money to take action. However if such farms were given to the CRT in Trust we would be happy to ensure the continuation of the farm and the sensitive farming methods.

The CRT's birth and infancy have exceeded all expectations. Now we want to spread our message, our acres and our practical work to new areas; our challenge is to keep the lark ascending.

41

Snowdon – The Fudging of the Countryside

I still feel disappointed at not buying Snowdon for the Countryside Restoration Trust. It is being purchased instead by the National Trust with the support of the Welsh Office, the Countryside Council for Wales, the Snowdonia National Park Authority, Uncle Anthony Hopkins and all. Helping to launch the Appeal to raise money, although why an organisation with a membership of 2 $\frac{1}{2}$m and an annual income of £180 m should have to launch a special appeal to raise £3 $\frac{1}{2}$m is a mystery. Chris Brasher, the well known manufacturer of walking boots, climbing boots and outdoor clothing said in triumph: 'We are challenging all the climbing and mountaineering clubs of Britain to come and match us pound for pound, because this is not just here to be able to feel the country (whatever that means), but it is also a great playground for the walkers and climbers.' So there it is, Snowdon and rural Wales with its people and culture is seen as a theme park – a 'playground', and hopefully all those walkers and climbers who respond to Mr Brasher's call will all be wearing 'Brasher' boots as they help to wear Snowdon down.

To help purchase this 'playground', Sir Anthony Hopkins is giving £1 m of his obviously hard earned money: 'We have less than a 100 days to save Snowdon,' he says in adverts placed in many national newspapers, including the DT. But 'save' it from what – people who regard it as more important than a playground? In his advert he also says: 'If we cannot raise those funds, this outstanding area may suffer from damaging commercial development and threats to its environment.' The CRT was planning to enhance the environment and being within a National Park, Snowdon is protected from 'damaging commercial development' by severe planning restrictions, so what are the National Trust and its famous actor on about – perhaps the Advertising Standards Authority should tell us?

When the Countryside Restoration Trust, of which I am Chairman, decided to put in a serious bid we were not bidding for 'Snowdon' or a theme park, and we had no wish to become playground monitors, we were bidding for two working hill farms which also welcomed visitors and tourists, and where visitors would still have been welcome. Our interest was to help improve a living and working countryside.

Our plans were exciting. We would have immediately stopped using sheep dips to avoid the problems of toxicity to both people and the land. Instead we would have used a spray, approved by the Soil Association, which I already use successfully on my sheep. Similarly we would have ceased to use any worming agent containing 'ivermectin' to prevent damage to harmless invertebrate populations. To offset the increased costs we would have helped the new tenants to market their lamb at a premium.

In addition to this we would have adjusted the rent according to the tenants' incomes. At the moment hill farms and in fact all farms are in crisis: incomes are dropping, yet rents are remaining static or even rising. In bad years we would have lowered the rent and in good years we would increase it. We simply do not understand why landowners and landlords (including the National Trust) do not do this already.

On the wildlife front the prospects were exciting, with a variety of habitats that could have been developed and improved. We would have kept sheep out of woodland to allow natural regeneration. Along the river and lakes we would have created otter havens by keeping livestock and people away from certain sections of bank and we would have experimented with waterside planting to try to improve spawning conditions for trout, salmon and sea trout. With a remnant population of black grouse it would have been a challenge to try to increase their numbers. Similarly we would have carried out a major effort to increase lapwing numbers; already the RSPB believes that its numbers are unsustainable. Reduced use of chemicals, fewer sheep and a purge on carrion crows, we believe, would rectify the situation.

In addition to this we would have put in visitor and educational facilities as we want urban visitors to understand where their food comes from and how it is produced. With an agenda like this we could have expected some interest from the numerous government agencies, quangoes, voluntary bodies and local officials. Astonishingly we got none; everybody was supporting the National Trust, before they had even heard of other schemes. The Taffia had struck.

Astonishingly, too, not only did the Welsh Office support the National Trust bid, but it also let it be known that if successful it would 'give' the National Trust another chunk of Snowdon. Why? And whose land is it for the Welsh Office to give away and under what authority? The intervention of the Welsh Secretary in the sale of these two hill farms is bizarre. Firstly it is direct government interference and pressure in a private sale, favouring one charity against another, and secondly the deal involves allowing fox hunting to continue on Snowdon. Thus, Mr Davies, outspokenly ignorant opponent of fox hunting, is supporting a scheme that allows it!

I have no problem with some aspects of the National Trust's work. It does some very good things particularly with great houses and stately homes. However some of its land management is poor. On National Trust holdings in the uplands it is possible to see overgrazing and overstocking at its worst, while on some of its lowland farms silage making goes on in May, the most crucial month for ground nesting birds and hedge cutting takes place in July and August. In fact if large land holding organisations such as the National Trust and the Church Commissioners farmed their land more responsibly there would have been no need for the formation of the CRT in the first place.

So another part of rural Britain is in the process of being demoted from living, working countryside to 'playground'. Never mind, I expect the inevitable National Trust Snowdon shop will sell plenty of waxed jackets and pot-pourri; it needn't bother with fudge, the area has plenty of that already.

42

The Sensible Season

As far as members of the media are concerned we are in the middle of the 'silly season'. It is the period when the politicians are on holiday during August and September; as far as I am concerned the absence of politicians makes it the 'extremely sensible season'. As far as the countryside is concerned however, the silly season now extends from January 1st until December 31st and it is rapidly becoming the 'very silly season'.

By far and away the silliest act this year, apart from the Government's attempted destruction of farming and the rural communities that go with it, was the release of mink into the New Forest by the Animal Liberation Front; don't these people ever learn, and won't these people ever learn? In the past I have written as a joke that some urbanites seem to believe that carnivores live on cucumber sandwiches and profiteroles. From the actions and self-justification of some animal activists it would appear that some may actually believe that the cucumber is the main diet of the mink. Indeed, judging from letters sent to the Press many bunny huggers believe that the average mink lives the life of a fur clad Buddhist monk.

One Sara Starkey claimed in the DT that mink eat 'vegetation', although all the books and experts that I have ever consulted suggest that the average diet of an adult mink is one third feather, one third fur and one third fin. In other words the mink menu is a tasty mixture of bird, animal and fish.

Another animal fantasist declared that releasing the mink was worth it for the 'euphoria' they would feel on achieving 'freedom'. I wonder if these same mink sit around contemplating such things as 'democracy', 'life after death' and 'free-market economics'. After the release of mink from cages it can only be a matter of time before these courageous and intelligent freedom fighters start releasing caged gerbils, hamsters and goldfish. We must just hope for their sakes that the euphoric gerbils, hamsters and goldfish do not meet the mink.

Fortunately the summer also provided me with an opportunity to meet sensible people who had been releasing creatures back into the wild. Butterfly Conservation, with invaluable help from ICI, has continued its work to re-introduce the large blue butterfly back into Britain. The large blue is one of our most spectacular butterflies and its drift into extinction was sad. The life cycle of the large blue involves ants, wild thyme and herb-rich grazed pasture. When myxomatosis decimated the rabbit population the grass became too long for the ants on which the large blue depended and so the butterfly disappeared. Now with sheep grazing and imported Swedish butterflies several colonies are again thriving in the West Country. Originally the butterfly was brought back to the edge of Dartmoor and it has since been helped to spread to a number of other sites. The one I saw was in Somerset; a wonderful south facing slope with ants, sheep and wild thyme. I saw the butterfly too which confirmed the success of the whole operation. Perhaps Butterfly Conservation should have a slogan proclaiming 'Eat Somerset Lamb and Help Save the Large Blue'.

Also on the site was one of my favourite butterflies, the marbled white. On the CRT land in Cambridgeshire it seems to me that we have created the ideal conditions for this beautiful butterfly. I must talk to Butterfly Conservation to see if they can extend a helping hand to that too. Marbled whites in our newly established 'traditional' hay meadows would make the experiment almost complete and demonstrate again the responsible side of 'animal liberation'.

An astonishing story comes from an English primary school. A pupil picked up a 'deadly fungus' on the school playing field. The child was rushed to Addenbrookes Hospital in Cambridge after touching such a hazardous object, where he remained perfectly fit and well; the school's annual sports day was postponed because of the threat to the school, pupils and parents and the playing field was sprayed with fungicide as a matter of urgency. At the end of the day the child was released, still perfectly fit and well and identification of the 'deadly fungus' came from the Plant Sciences Department of Cambridge University. It was a common, edible mushroom. I could understand such a over-reaction at an inner-city school, or a holiday home for neurotics – but this happened in a village on the edge of the Fens. So the hysterical city mind continues to colonise rural Britain.

After appearing on a television programme recently in which I explained the CRT's bid for the two hill farms in Snowdonia I was approached by a woman on Cambridge Station. 'Well done,' she said, 'I agreed with every word you said, we've got to keep Snowdon in England.' There was no answer to that.

After reading of the Snowdon saga a reader telephoned me with what he described as a true story. One day, he said, a little blind rabbit was hopping home when he bumped into a little blind toad. The toad touched the rabbit with its front leg and said: 'You've got nice soft fur; you've got nice twitchy whiskers; you've got long floppy ears – you must be a little bunny rabbit.' The little bunny rabbit put out a paw and said: 'You're very very cold; you are extremely slimy; you've got a very big mouth – you must be a land agent.' I must say that I simply cannot understand how such a joke should have materialised and I had to think twice before repeating it.

43

Farewell my Friend

———

Life takes many strange twists and turns. Already I have worn those shiny, black shoes again that I bought for the funeral of my closest friend, Gordon Beningfield; this time I have worn them for the funeral of my best friend – my father. (In fact I wore them twice in seven days as his elder sister died in the same week). His end came suddenly and unexpectedly; a short visit to hospital, an operation and he was gone. Another life on the land ended.

He had always wanted to farm, but at first his father did not take him seriously. My grandfather had left school to become a shepherd boy at thirteen, but then with a flair for business he had become a butcher with several shops in Cambridge. Consequently he wanted my father to follow in his footsteps for a life of cutting up carcasses and counting money. At school father had studied for business, in readiness for his rightful place in the family firm; he had learnt bookkeeping and accountancy and had gone through the butchery trade from top to bottom. He had scrubbed benches, made sausages, killed pigs, boned gammon and made brawn. He had then got married and announced that he intended to become a farmer. He had lived on the farm as a boy, and as mother's roots went back into the land for several generations, spreading out into the Fens, the idea appealed to both of them. It was not seen as a means of making money, but more as a way of life; a part of the eternal struggle for survival, which possessed far more dignity than selling mutton chops over a counter or sitting in a director's chair.

In wanting him to become a butcher, his parents had failed to take into consideration that their marriage had linked together two more extraordinary and independent families. Among their ranks had been abstainers and brewers, radical free-thinkers and blue-nosed Tories, churchmen and atheists, labourers and layabouts, and father had inherited idiosyncrasies from nearly all of them. The fact that he should insist on becoming a farmer against all their wishes was therefore not really in the least bit surprising.

He was a likeable mixture of diligence and dilatoriness, tolerance and turbulence, wisdom and wilfulness. He castigated his brother for being a member of the Conservative Party, but at the same time announced that it was impossible to be both a Christian and a Socialist. Later, when I became involved with the Referendum Party I expected mockery and indignation; I was flabbergasted as he embraced it with enthusiasm and when Jimmy Goldsmith flew into the village he greeted him like a long lost friend; on election day his Zimmer frame roared into top gear as he went to vote.

He referred to Freemasons as 'the forty thieves' and condemned profit; yet at the same time he joined the Country Landowners Association and lived by selling milk, eggs and corn for as much as he could get. He admired Oliver Cromwell but insisted that you could not mix religion and politics, and his Christian philosophy was in a constant state of flux, leaping the chasm from liberalism to fundamentalism and vice versa with amazing regularity and ease. When students came from Cambridge to preach in the village chapel they would be entertained to tea and supper and he would tease and torment them with his unorthodox views. It did them good however, and one has since become the Bishop of Coventry and another is Professor of Divinity at Durham University.

But to me, as a child, his contradictions went unnoticed; he was my father, a man respected, feared and admired. He taught me how to feed young calves, collect eggs without being pecked by broody hens, how to play cricket and bowl 'spinners' and by his example he showed me how to respect life. During times of disease or maternity he would sit for hours with the animals, helping, healing and encouraging, and he would demonstrate patience and understanding to them that he would not give to men. In return he was tossed three times by the bull and on one occasion he accidentally set a cockerel's broken leg the wrong way round. When the plaster was taken off the poor bird did not know whether it was coming or going.

In fact his whole mode of living was quite remarkable, for in effect he had virtually dropped out of conventional society. As he worked in the barn one day, wearing his dirty brown coat, a salesman waltzed in and asked: 'Where's the boss live, mate?' 'In the thatched house,' father replied. Minutes later the man was back: 'You are the boss.' 'I know. You asked me where I lived, so I told you.' He seldom went into Cambridge, he rarely had money in his pocket, appearance and prestige concerned him not at all, and because of this, as I grew older, I ceased to see him as a father-figure, but as a friend.

His life was the land and the seasons, and his harvest always included the wild harvest and the wildlife that shared the farm with him. We have buried him in his favourite meadow with the ashes of my mother next to him. Ashes to ashes and dust to dust; it was the resting place he wanted and he was carried there on a dray pulled by two shire horses. On his coffin was a wreath made from the wild harvest of the hedgerows and a sheaf of wheat from the farm, complete with a harvest mouse's nest woven into the stems. It was an appropriate farewell to a good and true countryman.

Both my mother and my father were familiar with the folklore of Cambridgeshire, because of the oral traditions that they grew up with. One of the old beliefs that they remembered was that if a robin came into the house it was a sign of a death in the family. I have been in my cottage for sixteen years and during that time it has been robinless, apart from me. On the Thursday before my father died I went to London; on my return I found that a quite unflustered robin had been shut in all day. On the Friday it was shut in again, quite unperturbed and in no hurry to leave. On the Saturday he died. On the warm days since, my doors and windows have been open as usual but the robin has not returned – strange but absolutely true.

44

Coming Home to Roost

The countryside is in crisis; the environmental disaster on our farmland caused by the Common Agricultural Policy has now turned into a major financial crisis, which in turn is becoming a social catastrophe. Prices are tumbling, thousands of farmers see no future for themselves and their families and there are feelings of bitterness and betrayal. From Devon to the Lakes I have met farmers who do not know what to do; some are angry, they want to block roads and march on London, while others have given up and I have seen strong men crying out of sheer despair.

The facts are simple; farm incomes are on the slide, not through the restructuring of farming or because of the naturally evolving economics of a modern agriculture, they have plummeted through a number of cynical political decisions taken under the Common Agricultural Policy, started by the last government and continued with an astonishing degree of glee and ignorance by the present one.

Sadly the leaders of the farming community must also be held partly responsible. Some of us have been warning for years that the CAP was a cul-de-sac that many farmers would be sucked into, but few would escape from still farming. Yet the NFU called, and many farmers followed, lured by short term feather-bedding and ignoring the long-term implications. Now the NFU feebly blames the 'strength of the pound' for the calamity it has supported, a claim that is nonsensical. Ten years ago the pound was stronger and farming was climbing up towards the crest of a wave. What has changed is not the strength of the pound, but CAP regulations and the government's attitude towards farming and the rural community.

Taking the price of agricultural goods as 100 in 1990 the fall in incomes is easy to see. In June this year the price of milling wheat was 75.4, milling oats 66.1, malting barley 77.4, sugar beet 97.1, cattle 81.9, pigs 80.7, milk 94.8 and eggs 82.7. Despite the drastic fall in all these prices I have not noticed a 25% drop in the price of biscuits, 20% in beer, 20% in beef and 35% in porridge. Food prices in the shops and supermarkets have remained the same, in other words the customer has been ripped off and the claim of the supermarkets to give the customer cheap food is ludicrous. At the same time virtually all costs to the farmer have risen. machinery now costs 125.6, machinery repair 145.2, cattle feed 109.2, etc.

The fall in cereal prices is simple. It has not resulted from the strong pound, but from the decision taken in 1992 to allow cereal prices within the EU to fall towards world prices as part of the GATT agreement (GATT in this case meaning Guarantees America Tripling Trade).

Even the crisis in pig farming, in which new piglets are being gassed at birth, is not solely linked to the strength of the pound. The supermarkets are buying the cheapest pork possible, often from countries without the same welfare costs as Britain, where medicines banned in Britain can still be used, where meat and bone meal are still fed and where traceability is not possible. In other words the supermarkets use one set of standards for the British farmer and another for their own profits.

On behalf of the CRT I recently requested a meeting with the new Minister, Nick 'Hovis' Brown, to express our concern at the environmental disaster linked to falling milk prices. All we received was an absurd letter from his Private Secretary, Mr Andrew Slade, stating that the Minister was too busy, and reeling out the usual claptrap that the fall in milk prices was due to the strength of the pound. This is nonsense; falling milk prices have nothing to do with the strength of the pound. Due to EU quotas Britain is not self sufficient in milk, and other EU countries cannot increase production to swamp the British market. In 1994 the Milk Marketing Board was scrapped by EU dictat in favour of the free market. It has been a disaster; prices have fallen and to stay profitable farmers are having to use their animals like machines and harvest grass from April to November, chopping up all the skylarks, lapwings and partridges as they go. 'Drinka Pinta Milka Day' advertising campaigns will never be used to boost consumption as none of the present milk buying companies want to run a campaign which may boost the consumption of their rivals.

All this flies in the face of the Government's fine words about environmentally friendly farming. There can only be conservation in farming, if there is profit to allow it. A farm failing financially will farm more intensively and farms going out of business will hasten the demise of rural culture; tragically a dying culture cannot be re-created. Evidently in multicultural Britain our rural culture is not wanted by an urban dominated Labour Government. Some weeks ago the CRT invited six ministers to look at and discuss farming's problems from a social and environmental aspect. We invited Messrs Blair, Cunningham, Morley, Rooker, Meacher and Prescott. The Prime Minister and Michael Meacher acknowledged and declined; the other four had neither the manners nor the interest to even acknowledge.

45

Cat Burglar

____

When I was a boy I swore that if ever I grew up I would never use the expression: 'When I was a boy'. Many people claim, quite wrongly, that I still have not grown up, yet I am saying 'When I was a boy' all the time these days. I make no apologies for using it again now, for when I was a boy one of the rarest species not just in the village, but in the county, was the ordinary, uncommon burglar. The farmhouse was never locked, equipment was never put away round the farm and crime was almost unheard of.

In a ring around the village five out of our six neighbouring villages had police houses, with policemen in them and a policeman was seen every day. More importantly, the policemen saw who was in the village daily and so they knew who should be doing what, where and when.

Since then policing has advanced, so we are told. The policemen have gone, the police houses have been sold off and a policeman on the beat is rarer than a sighting of the infamous Fen Tiger. As the policemen have disappeared so crime has rocketed and crime in the country is now as serious as that in the town. Unlike Ron Davies, those affected by crime do not feel guilty – they feel very, very angry.

But of course the police hierarchy, as well as those who rule us, tell us that crime is going down. With a mixture of political humbug, statistical manipulation and administrative mischief they claim that crime rates are falling, when those of us who actually live in the country know that the reverse is true. Even my local district council on which I have sat as an independent for 28 years, has joined the move towards misinformation, stating how crime is on the retreat – it is pure fantasy.

To celebrate the disappearance of crime our local community police officer has just been withdrawn, along with thirty others, to sit behind computers. She considered this to be a good career move as 'computer skills' are regarded highly by the Cambridgeshire Constabulary. The criminals appreciate the move too; the local golf club was recently broken into; my uncle's 4by4 went the same night; a friend's Range Rover then went missing, including his two Jack Russells inside and another friend's lurcher was stolen. When a farmer traced his horse trailer to a didecoy camp in Bedfordshire the police refused to go and retrieve it. Two days later it had disappeared completely. Didecoys – travellers – are now regarded as a 'minority group' in their own right and so have to be treated with kid gloves to prevent the wrath of the civil rights industry; the civil rights of those of us who live and work in the country are evidently unimportant.

Last week an expensive ride-on mower was hidden in a ditch

in one of the CRT's fields, presumably for collection later. When a police car arrived I suggested rather innocently: 'Why don't you set an ambush and get them when they come back for it.' 'You must be joking,' the policeman said: 'We are the only patrol car on duty at the moment for 56 villages.' If only it had been a computer in the ditch I suppose forty officers would have been immediately available.

Then came last Friday and the farmhouse, now locked religiously whenever empty, was burgled. I was there until 9.20 that morning; my sister returned at 10.45 to find papers all over the drive and the family's few heirlooms missing. Coming so soon after a year of bereavement she was heartbroken; all the old jewellery left to her by my mother had gone, as well as two small antique tables, a lovely little draught/needlework table, some china figures and a wonderful bronze tiger. They also stole her CRT gold coloured skylark brooch – worth £7.50. I am glad to tell them that all that glitters is not gold.

The furniture and the jewels were of great sentimental value and my old father loved to sit and play at the draught table. The tiger too will be missed; Japanese, it is both well cast and distinctive. It also has a claim to fame as it was once on The Antiques Roadshow with my mother giving its family history. If anybody sees it, or is even offered it, please let me know as soon as possible. For anybody giving information leading to imprisonment I will give a thousand pounds reward. I will give two thousand to the person who can arrange for the trial to be held in Saudi Arabia.

My mother was given the tiger just after the last war. The couple in the small-holding just down the road were leaving, and as an appreciation for her many kindnesses to them they wanted to give her the tiger. Mother was most reluctant to accept; she did good deeds for their own sake and wanted no reward. Alas she had no spare money to buy the tiger, so they struck a compromise. She would have the tiger, but in return they were to have a score of eggs for two weeks running: 'We used to often sell eggs by the score in those days.' So the tiger became a member of the family with its own little bit of history. It always attracted much attention – sadly now a little too much.

By coincidence, or design, another farmhouse, this time in the Fens has recently been burgled, just after a bereavement. If some criminals are targeting houses through the obituary columns then there are some very sick people out there who deserve to be rounded up and put away.

Evidently the Cambridgeshire Police have not been happy about me writing about their computer mania and an inspector wanted to talk to me about it. On phoning the number he gave out came this reply: 'The number you have dialled has not been recognised. The number . . . ': about par for the course it seems to me.

46

All I Want for Christmas

Father Christmas came early this year and gave me a present that I was most reluctant to accept – three false teeth. Yes the terrible news is that I have my first dentures – my first plastic replacements. Just as the first swallow is a sign of spring and fieldfares show that winter has arrived; the first false teeth seem to confirm Anno Domini.

It has been a traumatising experience as it has taught me that most people in this country are 'toothist' and it is surely time that Mr Blair brought in legislation to protect those of us who are dentally challenged. My problem started many years ago on the rugby field, when my sturdy, white, bright front teeth came into violent contact with a large solid cranium. Over the years one tooth was so damaged by that solid Peterborough skull that it dropped out, threatening to take two others with it; enter two crowns and a bridge. Sadly this solution was only temporary as the teeth continually dropped out at inconvenient moments, such as filming 'One Man and His Dog'.

The last straw came when they suddenly dropped out and sank to the bottom of my beer in the local pub. Women screamed and strong men fainted as they were confronted with gnashing gums and one solitary front tooth. I have never seen such a harsh reaction to misfortune and disability. Why people are horrified by bare gums I have no idea, but those of us with them are immediately ostracised; we become untouchable and our mental powers are assumed to diminish with toothlessness.

My initial reaction was to carry on. One front tooth was not inconvenient and in years gone by nearly everyone had teeth missing; but then came the invitation to speak at the Oxford Union, against the motion 'That this house wishes to ban all hunting with hounds immediately'. Could I go to debate at the Oxford Union with no teeth? This brought out the very worst toothist behaviour in those closest to me; not only was I told to get some teeth, but if I didn't I was threatened with being locked into my own house. In addition I was told that my moth eaten dinner jacket and bow tie would be auctioned off and the money donated to an orphanage for penguins.

So my dentist came up with a beautiful set of sparkling plastic gnashers that looked wonderful but could not bite their way into a spoonful of jelly. When I spoke I whistled, as a plastic denture has the same pitch as a sheep dog whistle and when I laughed my teeth almost dropped out. What should I do; how could I attend the pre-Oxford Union dinner, in case I swallowed the teeth? And how could I speak if my argument developed into a series of dog handling whistles? Then of course horror of horrors what would happen if the dentures flew out completely?

My three funniest memories at the village school in reverse order are – a little girl getting stuck in the lavatory, bottom down and legs up – for over an hour. The headmistress slamming a cupboard door which promptly fell off its hinges, and number one, that same headmistress shouting out in anger to gain control and her teeth flying through the air in a great arc; it caused total loss of control. How we laughed – was this now going to happen to me?

The problem nearly solved itself one evening as I was eating an orange. As no doubt many people do in their quiet moments,

I took the dreaded teeth out so that I could savage the peel with my solitary mighty striker. Half an hour later I realised that my teeth were missing. Three hours later I was still searching for them. Four hours later I found them, at the bottom of the dustbin bag with the orange peel. Oh dear, what's it going to be like in twenty years time?

Finally the great day dawned and complete with dentures and penguin suit I decamped to Oxford. During the dinner I only had to excuse myself once to sort out the dentures which were behaving like the Kon Tiki raft engulfed by a rough sea of half chewed cabbage. Then came the debate. I was convinced that we would lose and lose easily. How do you defend a pastime that few people come into contact with and fewer people understand?

Cool Britannia, is, in reality, urban and suburban Britain represented in Parliament by grey men with no culture. How would a new generation of aspiring debaters and politicians cope with the notion of 'uncool' hunting and a rural culture totally divorced from New Labour and its Euro-Millennium glitter? The answer quickly came; the anti hunters seemed devoid of humour, knowledge and conviction, whereas the arguments for hunting based on civil liberties, multi-culturalism and conservation remain as strong as ever. The great philosopher Roger Scruton demolished the antis so completely and so humourously that the motion was defeated by a clear hundred votes.

The whole process was interesting; the debate was really a game of scoring points and making cheap jibes, which brought the worst out of me. Facts were twisted, false interventions made and rowdiness rewarded. One student, the Union Treasurer, shamelessly distorted some of my wise words to his obvious glee. At the end of the debate I said to his father, 'With ability to twist words like that he should become a politician.' 'That is what he wants to be,' he replied proudly. Sadly that sums up politics today; it starts at Oxford and Cambridge as a game. The game continues in Parliament at our expense. Fortunately the players in the House of Commons still have not banned hunting and I will be at my local Boxing Day Meet, just as long as I can find my teeth.

47

A Christmas Carol . . .

We are at that time of year again; a time of hope and happiness for a vast army of bureaucrats. For there are many who see the approach of Christmas as a seasonal opportunity for muscle flexing and pedantry, all beautifully decorated with seasonal red tape and tidings of discomfort and joylessness. To most people the prospect of Father Christmas arriving with his reindeer is a time of excitement and happiness – the bureaucrat feels those very same feelings as he eagerly makes sure that Santa has filled in all the forms correctly relating to 'Health and Safety' and 'Risk Assessment'.

For years the Cairngorm reindeer have used the farm as a resting place between visits for Father Christmas and his reindeer, as well as for his small Scottish support crew. This year the tour of Rudolph and his friends has been as successful as always, but in places the support crew have been weighed down by forms. At first glance the contents of the forms seem most appropriate as jokes for Christmas crackers, but at second glance they are real, signed by real people, although I have a suspicion those responsible may have been genetically modified to accept the nonsense they have to administer.

Take 'Wigan borough partnership' (sic) for instance, an authority obviously fascinated by the blur of Blairspeak. As the day of Father Christmas's arrival approached, so the reindeer keepers were informed that the 'Borough Environmental Health & Safety and Consumer Protection Department' was concerned at the threat posed by the reindeer. The hapless keepers were informed that 'They (the health bureaucrats) have stated that unless they have confidence that the reindeer will not pose any threat to the health and safety of the public they may prevent the event from taking place'. So a risk assessment was asked for:

'What procedures are in place to ensure the reindeer do not bite or cause injury to members of the public?' What would they bite with I wonder, like most herbivores reindeer have no biting teeth at the front, only gums – perhaps 'Wigan borough partnership' was worried that people could be sucked to death.

> 'Could you please confirm the present state of health of the reindeer visiting Wigan Town Centre?'
> 'What condition are the reindeers (sic) antlers, i.e. Sharp, trimmed off etc?'
> 'How well trained are the reindeer?'
> 'Please supply the number of reindeer and ages'.
> 'What procedures or actions have you in place should the reindeer bolt or become loose?'
> 'How will you collect and dispose of any waste produced by the reindeer?' etc., etc.

Needless to say the visit to Wigan was a great success, no member of the public was savaged by a reindeer, although who cleared up the waste produced by nearby police horses is a mystery.

Consequently it seems almost certain that the Wigan 'Environmental Health & Safety and Consumer Protection Department' must be getting their red-tape in a twist over the arrival of Father Christmas on Christmas Eve. As a result I believe that the great man and his staff should be sent a risk assessment form immediately, and if they do not fill it in to the satisfaction of the Wigan borough partnership Father Christmas should be banned; any violation of Wigan airspace by an unauthorised flying sleigh should not be tolerated.

To preserve the health and safety of the whole of the North-West the questions the old man should be required to answer are:

> What procedures are in place in the event of Father Christmas becoming stuck in a chimney?
> Is his clothing made of non-inflammable material?
> What is the current state of health of Father Christmas – over-

weight? Too old? Senile dementia? A fear of flying?

Does his beard pose any unacceptable health hazard – dandruff? Eczema?

Is the beard securely fixed to avoid disappointment?

Has Father Christmas ever been prosecuted for incidents involving young children?

Is it true that Father Christmas is a compulsive liar?

Are his presents well secured to prevent them falling on the residents of Wigan from a great height?

Does Father Christmas have his own teeth or is he fitted with dentures? Will he bite?

How will you collect and dispose of any waste material produced by Father Christmas?

Does Father Christmas belong to a Trades Union?

Is he a member of any secret organisation?

What plans are in place in case Father Christmas bolts into the crowd or heads for the nearest off-licence?

Does he have a current heavy sleigh licence?

Do you have any contingency plans in the event of Father Christmas arriving the worse for drink?

What action will you take if 'Help the Aged Activists' disrupt his arrival?

Once the great bureaucrats of Wigan have frightened Father Christmas out of town they could prosecute carol singers for causing light and noise pollution and all those in nativity plays could be arrested for a variety of offences from cross-dressing; building a stable without planning permission and impersonating a camel. We are all so lucky to be living in super modern Cool Britannia at Christmas time. One more thought occurs, why not scrap 'Father Christmas' altogether and replace him with a multicultural, tri-sexual, smiling, benevolent Millennium Man, it could be called the Tone-Clone.

48

Partying with 'Hovis'

On the edge of Dartmoor a new form of hunting with dogs is apparently being allowed by this hunting-hating government. Men in hunting uniforms, with smiles on their faces, large dogs and guns are searching for a fierce and wicked lion. So wicked and fearsome is it that no damage to mice or men has been reported, but nevertheless it must die. Apparently the sightings of it were nowhere near a cider press so they are assumed to be real.

At the same time I have been trying to conduct a hunt of my own. I have been trying to track down the new Secretary of State for Agriculture, Mr Nick Hovis-Brown. Quite why Governments these days change their agriculture minister more times than a mole-catcher changes his long-johns in January is anybody's guess, but they do, and it remains to be seen whether or not 'Hovis' is as bad as all the rest.

Although Mr Brown has made much of his recent £120 million to livestock farmers, the truth is that due to the incompetent handling of BSE by both the last government and the present look-alike government, livestock farmers are many hundreds of millions of pounds down and thousands of farmers are teetering on the brink of bankruptcy due to the inept policies of those who rule us.

Hovis tells us that in delivering his package he has talked to a wide range of farming interests, but sadly he has refused to talk to me. Recently however I did get close to him. I never name drop, but when I was at the Palace the other day, for the Fiftieth Birthday of HRH Prince Charles, I apparently walked straight past Mr Brown as he stood in a corner. Sadly I mistook him for one of the waiters.

Then I nearly managed to talk to him on Channel Four News. I was invited to comment on Mr Brown's inadequate actions, and I was delighted to hear that Hovis would also be on. Sadly, he would only agree to appear if there was no discussion and so consequently I had no opportunity to put anything of substance to him. All he did was quote from his brief, prepared by the same dismal and non-comprehending civil servants who prepared briefs for John Seldom-Glummer, Douglas Hoggwash and Dr Jack Low-Cunningham. Never mind, the CRT will try yet again to see him. We will also invite him to our land in the spring and point out the differences between alder and elder, cowslips and cowpats – if there are any cows left by then.

The man I would like to see as Agriculture Minister is the one who held the party at Buckingham Palace – Prince Charles. It is ironic that a few years ago a clever-Dick Labour MP was attacking him for 'committing adultery' and 'talking to vegetables'; as far as I know HRH had never spoken to Ron Davies. Recent events in the wide open spaces of Clapham Common seem to be rather a case of the biter being bit.

I was invited to the Palace Party as Prince Charles is Patron of the CRT's Sir Laurens van der Post Memorial Appeal. It seems to me that he is a good man, much maligned and misunderstood, but streets ahead of our politicians when it comes to sensible environmental and social policies. From the hundreds of charities represented, it seems likely that he works harder than most MPs too.

Buckingham Palace is a wonderful place and so much better for having Royals in it, rather than ego-tripping failed politicians masquerading as Presidents. Imagine President Leon Brittan – what could be worse. My greatest pleasure at the party was almost treading on the Queen Mother. What a remarkable old lady; over the years I have acquired several royal personages as 'swops', but she was a first.

I wonder when our 'colleagues' in Europe will decide that our monarchy is too successful, attracting too many tourists and too much trade for Britain. Perhaps they have decided that already, hence all the nonsense about modernising the Monarchy. Queens on bikes seem to me to be most unappealing, and in any case we already have several of those in the Cabinet.

I hear that this was the real reason for the demise of the Royal Yacht *Britannia*. That our European colleagues considered that it gave us an unfair trading advantage when our Royals and high powered export teams arrived abroad. So it was our 'partners' who signed and sealed the sinking of the *Britannia* and our Prime Minister, 'Tone' willingly agreed to it – so boosting his chances of becoming the First President of 'Europe'. Apparently there are, or were, European minutes outlining the objections – I suppose they have gone the same way as European minutes highlighting the build up of BSE.

I recently had confirmation that I am totally unemployable. With the shambles that the Countryside Alliance found itself in after the retirement of the great Robin Hanbury-Tenison, I was approached by several people suggesting that I should throw my hat into the ring for the top job, as the Alliance has the potential to become the major pressure group for all countryside issues. Certainly I believe it should have been supporting the family farm at this time and organising a huge farmers' lobby in London. Farmers supported hunting when it was under fire, now, in an 'alliance' the hunters should be supporting the farmers. Out of two hundred applicants I got to the last three. On being questioned about fundraising I had to say that I wasn't interested and so life goes on as usual. I do believe mixing fundraising and policy is a major error, and they would have been surprised to know that I would only have done the job at half the ridiculous salary they were offering. I am not disappointed and I hope it works out for them this time.

49

Learning Curve

—

For years the agricultural policies of the CAP have baffled me. Never have the absurdities been so clearly demonstrated as last week when I was visited by a Kenyan, William Wapakala, of 'Farm Africa'. He was introduced to me by my local vicar, Canon Hugh Searle, a man well suited to my particular village, as he was once a prison chaplain.

In Kenya, William Wapakala works with the nomads and pastoralists of the North; it is an area I have visited many times and one of his projects skirts the Meru Game Reserve where George Adamson once had a camp for his lions. I was able to show William the Somali knife that I still have, swapped for my sheath knife with George's tracker Abdi.

Because of my visitor's keen interest in all things agricultural I drove him around our small family farm, as well as the land owned by the CRT; strange to relate, I believe that I learnt more from the experience than he did. The first problem came when I showed him our beef 'single suckler' herd. A single suckler is simply a cow that has one calf a year, and cow and calf stay together all summer. Looking at the fine udders, he asked reasonably: 'Do you milk them?' 'No,' I replied, 'we are not allowed to.' Coming from a country where all food is precious he looked baffled: 'Fancy not milking such fine healthy cows.' I felt that I could not go on to say that not only were we banned from milking them, but that our dairy herd was disbanded several years ago, along with countless others, specifically so that Britain would become a milk importer under EU regulations. William's 'third world' homeland was trying to become self-sufficient: we from the 'First World' were ordered to cease self-sufficiency!

Horror of horrors, next came the field of set-aside: sixteen acres

149

of absolutely nothing for which our tenant farmer is being paid over eighty pounds an acre. William looked bemused: 'You get paid for doing nothing?' 'Yes,' I had to admit, 'set-aside is a payment for not producing food.' He looked even more confused than he had on hearing that we did not milk the cows.

Then came our newly acquired flood plains that we had just sown with grass seed. This time I had to tell him that this sensible use of land was not by Government edict, it was on our own initiative to prevent nitrates and chemical residues getting into the nearby river system. I could not explain why this sensible move was not a government initiative, or why the absurd set-aside was. Nor could I explain why the government had failed to take all flood plains out of production, under set-aside, which would have been both logical and environmentally beneficial. Perhaps MAFF could give me the answer?

William explained to me that one of his schemes was to introduce Toggennburg goats from Britain to local tribesmen to improve the strain of goat and increase the milk yield. This he was pleased to say meant that with the increased yield more men were able to stay and work in the village instead of going off to the towns. I, on the other hand, had to explain that here in Britain the aim of increased production is the exact opposite; to drive people off the land, often from farms where a family had been working for generations, leaving them with no other option but to look for work in the towns. After our trip, not only was William clearly convinced that we were working a very strange system, but both me and the vicar were rapidly coming to the same conclusion.

The final irony came from the fact that his visit coincided with the announcement by MAFF that all 200 wild boar running loose in Kent were likely to be shot. We were worrying about a few roaming pigs, yet some of William Wapakala's pastoralists near Meru, are expected to put up with straying elephants, hippos and lions that wander from the game reserve next door. Each year several Africans get killed by wildlife, yet any suggestion of culling is greeted with howls of disapproval, not from Kenya, but thousands of miles away in comfortable, over-fed, paranoid

Britain. It is another example of totally distorted values; elephants are sacrosanct in Africa, where they cause us no danger, but all wild British pigs must be shot as soon as possible and no serious effort will be made to re-introduce them properly.

After our meeting and our trip, I think I was the one who had gained most – it had given me a clearer insight into the agricultural madness of the West. Ironically two people on the board of Farm Africa are the Europhiles Lord Plumb, MEP, a former President of the NFU, and Ben Gill the current President; I hope they never try to introduce CAP policies into Africa. It seems to me that the philosophy of Farm-Africa of self-sufficiency and healthy, working rural communities ought to be imported into Britain.

Hedgerow madness continues to flourish this year. Star turn is the Wawne Parish Council in East Yorkshire. Not only did the Parish Council grub up a hedge in full summer, incredibly because: 'it contains blackthorn, and is a danger to health'. But it seems that the hedge did not even belong to them and was protected by law. Now the Wawne P.C. refuses to discuss its own vandalism in public and the complacent East Riding District Council is not going to prosecute. For those wishing to help the hedgerow vandals, farmers, local authorities or whoever, at last the CRT's 'A Farmers' Guide to Hedgerow and Field Margin Management' is available.

50

DDT, BSE and Mad Advertisers Disease

———

For those of us linked closely to farming and who have been aware of genetic engineering over the last thirty years, the recent advertisements run by Monsanto, the American agro-chemical giant, have been disturbing. So much so that the CRT is complaining to the Advertising Standards Agency; after the scares of DDT and BSE we now have MAD – Mad Advertisers Disease.

Monsanto's approach is a carefully calculated soft-sell, in which everybody who expresses doubt or hostility is labelled a Luddite. In the CRT's case nothing could be further from the truth; we use much of agriculture's new technologies, but we do not like being misled. Ironically we are taking the Vegetarian Society to the Advertising Standards Agency too, for also making claims that we believe mislead the consumer. A recent Vegetarian Society advert implies that a vegetarian diet leads to less pollution; it slows global warming; it stops deforestation, etc. The advert conveniently forgets that rice fields are a major producer of greenhouse gases and that monoculture soya production is probably more polluting and leads to as much deforestation as cattle ranching.

However the vegetarian advert results from woolly, muddled thinking, while the Monsanto advert seems to be a determined effort to get acceptance for potentially harmful technologies. These could make Monsanto huge sums of money. Monsanto's claim is that by producing herbicide and insect resistant crops through genetic modification 'food (will be) grown in a more environmentally sustainable way, less dependent on the earth's scarce mineral resources'. Similar sorts of claims were made by the makers of the DDT-based seed dressings, insecticides and sheepdips of the 'Fifties and 'Sixties – their new chemistry was going to feed the world; instead it gave us Silent Spring and an environmental catastrophe that we are still recovering from.

BSE was another miracle of high-tech husbandry; a mixture of junk processed food and organo-phosphate chemicals used to control warble fly creating a devastating biological and economic cocktail. Once BSE appeared we were repeatedly told by politicians and scientists alike that there was 'no risk'. BSE apparently could not 'jump species'; overnight the reverse became true and the recent beef on bone ban took the hysteria to the opposite, and equally absurd extreme, thanks to the smug Dr Cunningham.

The truth is that some of the new biotechnologies are fraught with danger, yet scientists with vested interests are again reciting the 'no risk' mantra. Monsanto says in its advertisements 'we believe biotechnology is one way to cut down on pesticides used in agriculture'. To the layman this is fine, but the volume of chemical is irrelevant, it is the impact of that chemical that is important. Monsanto is breeding rape resistant to its own herbicide 'Roundup' – which incidentally the CRT uses responsibly on its land. Roundup kills most 'weeds'. Consequently the use of Roundup in a crop of rape is not addressing a specific problem it is spraying prophylactically. All 'weeds' will be eradicated, consequently not only will the crops be weed free, but also seed free, insect free, bird free and mammal free. The land will have the biodiversity of a billiard table, producing a dead countryside.

The CRT on its Cambridgeshire land is showing that the exact opposite is possible; that with sympathetic farming and specific treatment for specific problems high yields, quality food and abundant wildlife can be achieved. We are creating a living countryside, working with nature and not against it and helping to put the 'culture' back into 'agriculture'.

Ironically herbicide resistant crops can lead to more chemicals being used. The modified seeds left in the fields and growing up the next year ('volunteers') maintain their herbicide resistance; consequently they have to be knocked out with other sprays. In

Monsanto's case this means that Monsanto sells the Roundup resistant seed; it then sells the Roundup; it then sells additional sprays the following year to kill the 'volunteers' – what very good business! Pollen drift from genetically modified rape can then affect the orthodox crops of neighbouring fields and even cross with wild relatives such as the wild radish, or wild turnip, producing superweeds that cannot be killed with Roundup.

There are similar problems with plants that have been genetically engineered to resist or even kill insects. What happens if these genes escape into the general countryside affecting bees and other pollinators? The end result could be catastrophic with poor crops and few wild birds because of the lack of insects. Is this possible end product what Monsanto calls 'food grown in a more sustainable way'?

Sadly, one more gene is being played with by some companies – 'the terminator gene'. This gene stops second generation seeds from germinating, meaning that farmers cannot hold back some of their crop for next year's seed as it would not grow. As a result the chemical company has total hold over the farmer for both chemicals and seed.

At the moment Monsanto, along with others, is conducting a charm offensive in the Third World. The slogan is 'Let the Harvest Begin – the seeds of the future are planted. Allow them to grow. Then let the harvest begin. Because securing food for our future begins a better life for us all'. As it happens neither I, nor the CRT are against all biotechnology, however we are against folly, misrepresentation and exploitation. If Monsanto really is keen to feed the world why does it not concentrate on producing genetically engineered crops that will fix their own nitrogen – so saving both First and Third World farmers billions of pounds in artificial fertilisers; why isn't Monsanto transferring the drought resistant properties of millet and sorghum into wheat; why isn't it producing disease free cereals to prevent the use of fungicides; and if its ultimate aim is humanitarian, why isn't it making these life-saving technologies available to the Third World? In the opinion of a humble English peasant, I believe that Monsanto's motives are entirely based on profit and that a healthy, safe environment is more important than Monsanto's millions.

Logic would suggest that biotech research should be taken away from the chemical companies and should be undertaken at public expense for the good of food supply and a healthy world. Of course this country had such an establishment, at Cambridge – the Plant Breeding Institute – the PBI, with a worldwide reputation. With remarkable skill the Tories privatised it; they sold it to Unilever for £66 m in 1987 and it became Plant Breeding International (PBI). It is now on the market again; the price is expected to be over £200 m, and some believe that it will even make over £300 m. Those in the know are backing only one buyer – Monsanto.

51

The Bimbo Broadcasting Corporation

Last year something very strange happened, 'One Man and His Dog' was broadcast on Saturday afternoons at 4.30 on BBC 2 during January and February. The date is significant, because the broadcasts coincided with dusk; in other words the world's most well known sheep dog/country programme was shown at a time when most country people with sheepdogs were outside feeding and checking their livestock. Even I missed the only record that year of when I wore a tie. It was a good series, but I missed it and my video recorder is so complicated that I did not even bother to try and set it.

Sadly it appears that many other people were in the same boat; from Sutherland to Exmoor and from Ludlow to Little Snoring I was either asked why 'One Man and His Dog' had been shown at such an absurd time, or I was told that it had been missed altogether and why had it been taken off. Indeed at the Suffolk Show one old man got so irate that he seemed to blame me personally for the demise of his favourite programme; he simply would not believe that I carry about as much weight with the BBC as Tony Blair with the Muslim Institute of Peace Studies.

To try and find out why the BBC had broadcast the series when so many devotees could not watch I decided to write to the BBC, and I also wanted to know if the transmission time had been a device to reduce viewing figures in order to get rid of the programme altogether. To find out the answers I wrote to the then controller of BBC 2, Mark Thompson. After a long wait, all I received was a vacuous letter from the Viewers and Listeners Complaints Department. When I phoned to say yes, I was a viewer and a listener, but I was also the Presenter of 'One Man and His Dog', the lady apologised profusely and assured me that I would hear from the Controller within a fortnight.

Six months later I had still heard nothing. I know that I am the very worst person to criticise those who fail to answer letters, as I find it very difficult to deal with the several thousand that I get each year, but then I don't have banks of secretaries and PAs and I have to buy all my own stamps. Not only did the failure to reply seem rude, but it also seemed to confirm the way in which rural issues and rural people are ignored. As a public service organisation the BBC seems to cater for most minorities, but our own rural minority does not seem to count and in the much heralded 'multi-cultural' Britain, rural culture seems to be under almost constant attack.

Worse was to follow; as I waited in vain for the Controller to reply I heard that the current series of 'One Man and His Dog' was again going to be broadcast through January and February at dusk on BBC 2, guaranteeing once more that all those with sheep and cattle cannot watch. When coupled with the other country output from the BBC – from the suburban 'Countryfile' to the trendy 'Tracks', it does seem that real country people and real country issues are being sidelined.

Out of frustration and desperation I directed a missive at the BBC's Director of Programmes, Alan Yentob. Again silence followed. Ironically, during the pause I received a letter from

Switzerland, saying how much the Swiss were enjoying 'One Man and His Dog'. Then a message arrived saying that the programmes were going to be shown in America twice a week. It seems the whole world likes to see sheep and sheepdogs on television, except British programme planners.

Suddenly one Thursday the phone rang. The voice said 'Alan Yentob here'. I almost replied: 'Yes and I'm the Queen, what can I do for you?', but fortunately I refrained. It really was Alan Yentob, and soon I will be going to the bowels of Broadcasting House to discuss the issue of the countryside on television – at least it's an issue for those of use who live and work in the countryside and who seem to spend all our time fighting for its physical and cultural survival.

Some time ago I made the rather obvious comment that in its current affairs programmes, the BBC had come to be known as the Brussels Broadcasting Corporation. Now from some of its 'entertainment' output I am told that it should be known as the Bimbo Broadcasting Corporation. Recently it is alleged that a Bimbo was trying to show that some blondes do have intelligence. 'I can name the capital of every county in Britain,' she boasted. 'Alright then,' she was challenged, 'what is the capital of Warwickshire?' 'W,' she replied in triumph.

For Christmas I was fortunate to receive a bottle of wonderful Somerset Apple Brandy; on a cold winter's day it warms up every extremity and gets to the parts instantly that would take Heineken many pints. Obviously the Somerset Cider Brandy Company also makes cider. It makes sparkling cider in the traditional, natural way and it is at the craft end of the cider market. It is made from English cider apples, grown in Somerset and it ferments and is pressurised in the bottle. Because of this it has to have a mushroom cork to cope with the pressure. Ordinary cider on the whole is cooked, carbonated and sweetened, using imported apples and is virtually an industrial process.

From next spring new regulations coming from Brussels and implemented by Parliament will increase the duty on this craft cider by up to 500% and £1.40 a bottle – 20% above the finest claret. Because only the equivalent of two road tankers of this wonderful cider is made a year the tax officials and members of parliament seem uninterested in the plight of this small part of our rural economy and culture. 'Countryfile', when are you going to ride to the rescue? You are late as usual.

52

Farming for the Future

This year sees work starting in earnest to restore the land purchased in 1998 by The Countryside Restoration Trust, with invaluable help from the Heritage Lottery Fund. When the lottery started I was one of those cynics who believed that it was simply an extension of gambling, with few benefits to ordinary people. I was wrong; when College Farm came on the market for the first time since 1342 the staff at the Heritage Lottery Fund could not have been more helpful. The CRT had to compete for the land on the open market, within the restrictions of the lottery rules, and we received every help and encouragement for our scheme, which the Heritage Lottery Fund recognised as both exciting and important.

From our perspective, the purchase of the 140 acres from Corpus Christi and St Catherines was vital; the land was right next to that already owned by the CRT and it would turn our holding from a 'plot', of 95 acres, to a farm of 235 acres. With that purchase College Farm became The Sir Laurens van der Post Lark Rise Farm.

Once all the documents had been signed and sealed we did not change the farming regime. The land had already been cultivated and sown and we continued to farm it intensively with a maximum use of chemicals and fertilisers. It was literally a prairie of wall to wall wheat and rape and we wanted to monitor the land as an 'intensive farm', to find out what wildlife was managing to survive with hardly any habitat and regular applications of pesticides and nitrates. By doing this we would then be able to measure the changes in wildlife populations once the type of farming changed.

Both volunteer and professional monitors worked throughout the summer checking the populations of birds, butterflies, plants, mammals and invertebrates. The results have been depressing, with few species, and most of those surviving being saved by the banks of an old ditch that had managed to retain a surprisingly wide range of plant life and even a small population of harvest mice. The land held a few larks, and its large fields attracted a handful of English partridges, but on the whole the 140 acres was dead. It grew crops to a modern standard; but from a farming and wildlife point of view it was a disaster.

Already we are changing the regime. Fortunately Lark Rise Farm fell into one of the Government's new Arable Stewardship Pilot Schemes. Despite opposition from Gordon Brown, Elliot Morley backed and won the argument over this important new initiative. Its aim is to re-direct subsidies away from production, towards the means of production. Consequently our tenant farmer Tim Scott has agreed a scheme involving winter stubbles, spring sowing of wheat and barley, undersowing wheat with grass, grass margins, unsprayed headlands, beetle banks, wildlife strips, hedges and woodland. It is an exciting prospect and over the next five years we should see the landscape and the wildlife change dramatically, while at the same time good quality food will still be grown. We see this as the way forward for farming, with subsidies rewarding and encouraging environmentally friendly farming and quality food. Already the grass margins have been sown; beetle banks created and volunteers are planting the hedges.

Over recent weeks the Worldwide Fund for Nature and various other bodies have been delivering gloomy predictions of extinction and asking for changes in wildlife protection. We are showing that these predictions are too gloomy and that new legislation is not required, just a new approach to farming and an

159

urgent dismantling of the present eco-unfriendly Common Agricultural Policy: reform of the CAP is not enough.

Our scheme has been made even more pioneering as we have been linking the new Arable Stewardship Scheme with the already established Countryside Stewardship Scheme. Our purchase extends our ownership of the little brook where otters returned so memorably five years ago and we are again turning the flood plain into traditional meadowland. This time our seed source has been slightly different. Still using Miriam Rothschild's inspiration, methods and advice we have collected our own seed. With help from the Farming and Wildlife Advisory Group we located a traditional farm near Huntingdon with old grassland. The Meadowlands Trust harvested the seed for us and we have planted one of the meadows with this mixture.

Going even more local, we used a Novartis trials combine to harvest the grass seed from The Leys, my own village green, just a mile from the land. So seed of local provenance has been planted in the parish and one of the rarest farming habitats in Cambridgeshire, old grassland, is being grown again on a restored flood plain. Not only will it provide grazing and hay but it will also prevent nitrates and pesticide drift getting into the Cam River system.

In going for Arable and Countryside Stewardship there have been both positive and negative sides. The officials running the Arable Stewardship Scheme have been helpful, efficient and enthusiastic, and agreements were finalised in mid-summer. Sadly some of the officials dealing with Countryside Stewardship have been pedantic, bureaucratic and unimaginative. Amazingly too, some agreements are still not signed and the CRT's agreement was not ready for signature until the end of September – so we missed the best conditions for planting our grass. If farmers are to be encouraged to appreciate environmentally friendly farming they must be able to plan their year, and agreements should be ready for signing in June, to enable the proper planning of autumn cultivations and work. The officials must also be flexible, use common sense and smile.

Copying Highgrove's example the CRT wanted to mimic a

sheep drove across its land – a green lane with a hedge either side. The bureaucrat in charge allowed one hedge – 'two hedges will spoil the view for walkers'. A hedge containing numerous species of tree and shrub spoiling the view? It is beyond reason.

The mammal survey of the new land conducted by Dr Bob Stebbings has been most worrying. It revealed plenty of brown hares and two badger setts but no field voles, water voles, water shrews, hedgehogs and bats. Field voles are vital to many predators – kestrels, barn owls, tawny owls, etc, and I never imagined that the hedgehog would disappear. Not one bat indicates a disturbing lack of both habitat and insects. I wonder if the absence of bats also helps to explain the decrease in swallow numbers? There is simply not the food to sustain them.

The mammal survey did uncover one interesting incident on the Trust's old land. During the Easter Floods a large chub became stranded in the pond dug out for dragonflies. Whenever I went to the pond I saw this enormous fish; every time Mick Brown, a volunteer fisherman, went to catch the monster, to return it to the brook, he could never see it. In late summer another fisherman caught it. It finished up as a pile of bones and scales at the water's edge with otter paw marks next to it. The fish was so big that it looked as if it had been dragged out of the water.

The ultimate aim of the CRT is to have a network of environmentally friendly farms throughout the country linking farming and wildlife and extending the work pioneered by the Game Conservancy to benefit all wildlife. The farms will be setting a new agenda for farming, and making a profit – conservation cannot succeed on farmland without profit.

53

Axed

———

Oh dear, I'm unemployed again. Yes, the BBC has let it slip out that after the completion of the present series, in mid-March, there will be no more 'One Man and His Dog'. So after twenty-two years, with millions of followers and admirers throughout the world – Denmark, Holland, Sweden, Switzerland, the USA etc – 'One Man and His Dog' is being axed without so much as a thankyou to presenters, producers, competitors, sheep or dogs.

Although typical of the current BBC management culture, the axing is ill thought out, ill mannered and yet another example of the dumbing down and political correctness of the Beeb. Consequently the BBC is turning from an important medium for information, education and entertainment, into a private club that allows the chosen few to flaunt a tedious mixture of trivia, trendiness and trash.

The sad passing of 'One Man and His Dog' actually affects me very little, although I expect writing this Diary will exclude me from any future work, labelling me as a 'troublemaker'. It is only the politically correct whose views represent the search for truth and 'free speech'.

I regarded it as both a privilege and a pleasure to present the programme, which I believe still should have a place in the schedules and shows the BBC at its best; producing a quality pro-gramme for a minority interest; in this case the rural minority, which also attracts many sympathetic urban viewers. This repre-sents one of the highest aims of 'public service television'. The poor rate of pay and the exposure given made it almost irrele-vant in my working year – but I was happy to give up 2 ½ weeks a year for a section of the community which eagerly looked forward to 'their' programme. Well, to be entirely accurate, I was happy until the present series; Television Centre is now in such a shambolic state with production facilities being made into executive suites, that we had to record the 'voice-overs' in a converted garage in Watford!

The decision to scrap 'One Man and His Dog' could not have come at a worse time for that part of the community it both represents and serves – the beleaguered livestock farmers and rural communities in our upland areas; men and women often isolated physically and socially and now under considerable financial attack through no fault of their own. These farmers, shepherds and country people regarded 'One Man and His Dog' as 'their' programme, and now, at a stroke, they have been sidelined by the BBC's out-of-touch, over-paid, centralised London elite. So the countryside is under attack again, this time from its own broadcasting service. As one seasoned non-London BBC producer commented to me this week: 'The rural community? They (the BBC executives) don't give a damn.'

'One Man and His Dog' was originally screened as a 'one-off'. The idea of the then producer Philip Gilbert. So great was the impact that it came back by popular demand. Viewers liked its simplicity, the beautiful surroundings and they felt as if they were being given a real taste of country life. Viewing figures soared to 8 million; it followed 'Pot Black' and was in the safe hands of Ian Smith the producer and Phil Drabble the presenter.

On Drabble's retirement I was asked to take over as presenter, in 1994, and teamed up with other newcomers, Gus Dermody as commentator, and Joy Corbett the producer. Soon it became clear to me that 'One Man and His Dog' 's days were numbered. The day and time of transmission were moved until last year when it was shown, quite absurdly, on Saturday afternoons. It was obvious that an attempt was being made to reduce viewing figures to oust a popular and good programme that was no longer 'sexy' enough for BBC 2's controller. The People's BBC should become the UBC – the Urban Broadcasting Corporation.

So the same absurd slot was given to it this year. Following my telephone conversation with Alan Yentob, Director of Broadcasting, I met Nicholas Moss, Head of Policy, last week. He was a pleasant man, but he let the information slip that the new controller of BBC 2, Jane Root had already decided not to recommission the programme, before she had even seen the viewing figures. This was despite an assurance to the programme's producer that no decision would be made until the end of the series.

'One Man and His Dog' is the only programme on all channels rooted completely in the country and with viewing figures of 1.6 million it comes close to matching those obtained by the suburban 'Countryfile' (1.5–2 million) on BBC 1.

All this makes the BBC's position difficult to understand. Gus Dermody my colleague is disappointed for the hill men. As he scanned ewes from a snow covered barn during the week he said: 'As I go from farm to farm I am continually being asked: "What is the future of 'One Man and His Dog'?" They are really upset by the change of time and day. They can't watch it because of the time and believe that the BBC is trying to get rid of it. They feel under attack from the BBC. If it goes it will leave a great void both at home and abroad – our shepherds and sheepdogs deserve better.'

Chris Todd a hill farmer in the middle of the Lake District is equally upset. He is a former runner-up in the brace competition and spoke to me after coming in from the hills, covered in snow. 'It's a shame as far as we are concerned, most of my neighbours and fell farmers watch it. The hikers that walk past always comment on it – they reckon it's a proper country programme – but it's at such a silly time to watch. The hikers are out in the hills and the farmers are out with their livestock.' From the Yorkshire Wolds, near Driffield, Neil Jones, a competitor in the current series is equally disillusioned: 'I am very disappointed. They would have had a better following if "One Man and His Dog" had been shown at a more sensible time. For country people carrying on their normal lives during the daytime it's most inconvenient. Anybody with livestock, or even out walking are busy when the programme is on.'

Even those not directly involved in the programme are saddened by the loss. Ben Gill, the President of the NFU, says:

'The success of the BBC programme "One Man and His Dog" has underlined the enormous interest that the British public has in rural affairs. The programme has turned what for many was a rural activity of little interest into something much more real. At the same time it has brought into our homes the true story of those involved in the everyday life of the livestock farmer. Ending the series would leave a major gap in our future generations' understanding of rural livestock farms and countryside issues.'

For the new Chief Executive of the Countryside Alliance, Richard Burge, the news was greeted with disbelief, as it is one of his favourite programmes. 'This is a major piece of bad news,' he complained, 'If ever there was a clear example of the intimacy of the relationship between man and animals, it is "One Man and His Dog". In the spirit of its ongoing initiative "The BBC Listens", I hope the organisation will listen to the countryside and review its decision. This programme is an important example of how the BBC can help urban communities understand the way of life of rural Britain.'

Strangely, Mike Ward, Head of Events, the BBC department that makes 'One Man and His Dog', has not been told officially why the programme is to go. 'I suppose there is a feeling it has run its course and maybe it's time for a change. All things must come to an end eventually. The challenge is to create a country programme that will run for the next twenty years.'

To get the official version for the death of 'One Man and His Dog' I applied for an interview with the Controller of BBC 2, Jane Root. This was refused, but just as I completed this Diary I was given a statement from her office: 'The new Controller is looking at the future of the programme. A final decision will be made soon.' So it looks as if a re-think is still just possible.

From its own 'The BBC Listens' propaganda the Corporation says: 'We believe the BBC is getting much better at listening to audiences and hearing what they are saying about programmes,' From this it is quite clear that several BBC executives ought to have their ears syringed out with hot, soapy water.

Unfortunately being sacked is not a new experience for me. At school I was thrown out of the Combined Cadet Force for being allergic to manic, spotty adolescents pretending to be officers. At Nottingham Teachers Training College I was thrown out for being allergic to the educational clap-trap of the 'Sixties. In 1969 I was thrown out of the National Assistance Board for being allergic to the misinformation given out by Richard Crossman MP and David Ennals MP. Both were later given peerages for their services to our warped political system. In 1991 I was even sacked by *The Daily Telegraph*, with no reason given, so beating my colleague Willy Poole by several years. Fortunately we were both soon invited back. In 1997 I was sacked from BBC's 'Question Time' for joining the Referendum Party. I was simultaneously dropped from 'Any Questions', presumably for the same reason – I wasn't told and I didn't bother to ask. Long live the British tradition of free speech for one and all.

54

Dog Bites Back

———

I am writing this Country Diary bleary eyed, in a state of near exhaustion. I want a holiday, but then a flicker of memory tells me that I had one last month. A glass of port and a giant slice of coffee cake would also be welcome, to refresh both mind and body, but sadly I have given up everything, yes everything I like, for Lent.

The reason for my current state is you dear reader – thousands of you, and I thank you all most sincerely. The response to my last chapter has been astonishing; it has been like living on another planet – Pluto or even Uranus. As soon as some of you read that 'One Man and His Dog' was being assigned to the BBC dustbin, you began to write letters of anger and outrage and the trickle turned into a deluge. It was quite clear that a huge number of people felt that the Beeb had lost the plot, and said so.

When the *Telegraph's* campaign to save the programme spilled over into the rest of the media, with the notable exception of BBC television, I became totally overwhelmed by an avalanche of letters, faxes, phone calls and people banging on my door. As I rushed from room to room trying to find my half-moon glasses to read yet another fax, I suddenly found them; one pair was hanging round my neck and the spare pair was already perched precariously on the end of my nose.

When checking my sheep I had to wave, rather like the Queen to passing cars, and from their reaction I suspect that even the sheep realised that some great drama was being played out involving them, or their relations. One car stopped and the driver asked enthusiastically: 'Is your brother the one on television and in the paper?' His glasses were larger than half-moon, but obviously not large enough. At one time I took refuge in my roof, to escape the phone and write this article. In the living room was a pleasant American lady journalist from the *Independent* writing a piece on her computer, while Sky engineers were preparing my study for a live broadcast to the nation, using a giant mobile satellite dish parked in the road. It was all rather like a special edition of 'Monty Python's Flying Circus'.

My greatest achievement I suppose was to make the front page of the *Sun*, actually spilling over on to page three. However, I did manage to keep my shirt on, and my nipples suitably concealed. I learnt something about tabloid journalism too; yes I was pleased that the *Sun* added its voice to all the others, but did I really say 'Thank you, my Sun'; somehow it does not quite sound like me and the reporter suffered an acute attack of deafness when I said 'I would prefer "One Man and His Dog" to stay on terrestrial television if possible; however . . .'

Then the BBC's Chief Executive Will Wyatt became involved, praising the BBC's countryside output and saying 'We are the only broadcaster with a commitment to rural affairs'. This led to another batch of letters asking why, in view of this commitment, 'Farming Today' is broadcast at 5.47 am – hardly prime time radio. 'Countryfile' too came in for criticism through its often urban interpretation of countryside issues. Putting urban journalists on country matters is rather like getting the Ku Klux Klan to write about race or getting Mike Tyson to present 'Crimewatch' and Julian Clary to introduce 'Songs of Praise'.

Then came information from within the BBC itself asking why, if the BBC's commitment to rural affairs is so great was the BBC's Rural Affairs Unit, in Birmingham, disbanded last October? Countryside matters are now evidently a small part of the Factual and Music Department – presumably coming in the list of priorities somewhere after Eisteddfods and Folk Festivals. In addition a total of five experienced producers and assistant producers have just been given their marching orders by 'Countryfile'.

In local radio phone-in programmes, from all over the country, the switchboards were jammed – with about 98% wanting to keep 'One Man and His Dog'. Then Chris Smith the Culture and Media Secretary joined the fray on 'Any Questions'.

On Monday I called at the *Weekend* offices to take charge of two sacks containing an amazing 3,500 letters, and since then hundreds more have continued to pour in. They were so heavy it was like trying to carry two fat lambs over my shoulder. On arriving at Television Centre to deliver your mail I was both surprised and partly reassured to be invited in, from where I was directed inwards and upwards to the dizzy heights of BBC Controllerland. There I met both Alan Yentob, Director of Broadcasting, and Jane Root the new Controller of BBC 2.

We had a civilised and amiable discussion and another one was promised. They both spoke and listened and I believe that there has been some movement; perhaps in one form or another 'One Man and His Dog' can be saved and if that happens I believe it will be because of the massive response by *Telegraph* readers – and keep those letters coming in.

I believe that the BBC has been both surprised and jolted by the strength of feeling of the general public and the way in which the *Telegraph* was joined by virtually every other newspaper: except the sad old *Guardian*, whose circulation figures make 'One Man and His Dog' viewing figures seem like 'Top of the Pops'. But then the *Guardian* never has been noted for its countryside awareness. Just before the BSE crisis broke in 1996 the *Guardian*'s Editor famously commented that 'BSE is not an issue'. Hopefully the Beeb has seen that a lot of people have lost faith with its coverage of the countryside, and it has actually lost touch with a large chunk of its audience.

Interestingly in a recent poll on why people liked living in Britain, first, with 50%, came free speech (somewhat of an illusion. I was dropped by both 'Question Time' and 'Any Questions' before the last election. My crime, according to a producer – joining the Referendum Party). Second, with 40% came the appeal of the British countryside. It seems that the BBC still has not realised just how important it is to so many people.

Despite the astonishing response I have been left with feelings of both sorrow and bewilderment. In 'Country Diary', both Willy Poole and myself deal with many serious issues, and we both get an incredible stream of informed letters from readers. Some of these issues are fundamental to the whole future and structure of the countryside and go far beyond television programmes. They concern the tragedy of our upland farms; the destruction of our slaughterhouses; BSE and the ridiculous T-bone steak ban; the environmental, social and economic disaster of the CAP; the never ending attacks on our rural traditions; the threat to our rural culture in a supposedly multicultural society, etc, etc. . . . If only the rest of the media would joint us in fighting these battles too. Sadly the attack on 'One Man and His Dog' is a symptom of something far deeper and more disturbing – the gradual demise of the countryside as we know it.

Because of all these things the Countryside Restoration Trust recently wrote to each of our 659 MPs concerning the current countryside crisis. Although it is thought that over 200 MPs (30%) are expected to sign an Early Day Motion about 'One Man and His Dog', only 18 (2.75%) replied to the CRT about the real issues, with another 21 MPs sending acknowledgements. Let us hope that the *Telegraph*'s campaign will not only awake the BBC to the needs and issues of the countryside, but that our MPs can be stirred from their indifference and stupor as well.

55

Bramble on a Ramble

———

The other day I almost became One Man Without His Dog. Just beyond my back garden I have bought a small five acre field. It does not belong to the CRT, I bought it for myself. I want to carry out a variety of experiments on it, all of which would horrify Monsanto, and so I am wasting my own money and nobody else's. As I was busy planting an old fashioned greengage tree, genetically and politically unmodified, I heard a spine chilling scream of an animal in distress. I stopped and listened, baffled; then it came again, it sounded as if it was coming from my garden.

I tried to run but the heavy clay was sticking to my wellies in great balls and so my sprint became a waddle. As I crossed the ditch the sound of anguish became worse and there it was, Bramble, my faithful long haired lurcher was totally tangled up in a bramble bush. The more he struggled the more ensnared he became and blood was coming from a gash on his head.

He was becoming desperate and even when I tried to calm him he struggled on. Fortunately, although a growing number of people believe that all guns and knives are offensive weapons, I had my knife in my pocket. I grabbed the brambles, (the plants) with one bare hand and hacked at them with the knife held in the other. In no time Bramble was free, leaving both my hands bleeding far worse than his head. He calmed down quickly and soon was none the worse for his ordeal.

The poor old boy had obviously intended to follow me to the bottom of the garden, but with sight and hearing not quite what they used to be he had got thoroughly caught up by his namesake. He has been a good friend and companion since he was a puppy, but soon, I fear, I will be faced with that awful dilemma – when does an old dog become an unhappy, suffering dog? Whenever the vet comes to the farm I get him to check Bramble, to make sure that he too believes that my old dog is still enjoying life. But if he begins to suffer, then I will have him helped away peacefully; a friend deserves nothing less. Isn't it strange how we give our dogs far more respect and considera-tion than we give our human friends and relations?

The furore from 'One Man and His Dog' continues to have a life of its own. As a result I was recently offered the highest accolade that modern Western society can offer – I was asked to take part in an advert. I was excited; what was it to be? My favourite chocolate? Beer? Or, as my image is genteel perhaps it would be 'fragrance for countrymen – use muckspreader deodorant to-day. You too can be the smell of the countryside'. Sadly it was for none of these things; yes, you guessed, it was for sheep dip; not the Sheep Dip malt whisky, but real chemically improved sheep dip. The agency was rather astounded; instead of taking the money – over three times the rate for 'One Man and His Dog' – I asked them for a list of the chemicals used before deciding.

Then came an invitation to discuss the Countryside on Newsnight – yes mainstream BBC television at last. On arrival I was approached by a gentleman chewing gum with the open mouthed elegance of a football manager. 'Who are you?' he asked. 'Who are you?' I replied, 'chewing like that you must be a football manager.' I was wrong, he was Gordon Brewer, the pre-senter. I was grateful to him however, as I have been puzzled for years by the growing habit of chewing gum with open jaws and slapping lips, rather like a monitor lizard eating entrails. Of course the man with the greatest style, whose mouth opens widest and fastest is Alex Ferguson, the Manchester United manager. So why do these people do it? When I played village football I never needed to chew, and when I watch Cambridge United I need valium, not gum and medallions – so does gumming serve any real purpose apart from creating I presume, a macho image? Perhaps that will be my next advert – chewing gum without losing my teeth. The big question is, do gum chewers chew in the same way when they are invited out to dinner; if they do then the carpet and tablecloth must need dry cleaning after every meal. No football manager or television presenter will ever be invited to sit at my dinner table, until I know the answer.

The discussion took the usual form – Sean Rickard, who has advised the NFU, Government and yes, the BBC, was wheeled out to recite the nonsense that has caused the current crisis in agriculture – efficiency, competitiveness, the wonders of globalisation etc. After 2000 years, apparently all most people have learnt is that if something makes money, it is 'efficient' and good. If it does not make money it is 'inefficient' and bad. Perhaps the roof of the Millennium Dome should be decorated with a giant pound coin, the sign of our new God.

Sadly, this whole philosophy is now up for discussion at the CAP talks. This much hyped meeting about 'Reform' and 'Agenda 2000' is all hype. Remember you read it here first – the so called reform will be no such thing. Overall, CAP spending will go up; virtually all the subsidies will be production led, as now, and there will be no more money for agri-environment schemes – despite all the Government's pre and post election waffle. Any slight savings on top of subsidy payouts will simply be absorbed elsewhere.

The only good thing about the talks, senior officials tell me, is that at last Tony Blair will have to sit down and discuss countryside issues – for the first time since the Countryside March. Apparently he is said to be the most ill-informed and uninterested Prime Minister ever on rural affairs. It is even believed he may have to have picture cards to help him through the discussions – a cow, a turnip – 'Does that mean turnips come from cows?' 'No, let us explain, Prime Minister . . .'

56

One Man Without His Dog

It is the end of a chapter; I have now lost my most loyal friend. The vet came and my little lurcher Bramble slowly and peacefully drifted out of my life. It is a strange and inexplicable thing that even after two years of important and significant losses, the parting of my dog has caused me just as much sorrow as all the others. I suppose a psychologist would come up with some bright, trite explanation; all I know is that he was a real friend and half my visitors came to see him and not me.

There are a great variety of dogs; large, small, fat, thin, aggressive, submissive, lazy and hyper-active. Bramble was essentially a happy little dog. Even those who professed not to like dogs were soon totally under his control. I have always been fascinated by running dogs and the people who own them. A nearby gypsy always had lurchers and wherever he walked with them the rabbit and hare population immediately plummeted.

But although fascinated by lurchers I had never imagined owning one until I met the retired headkeeper at Sandringham, Monty Christopher. He is from the old school of gamekeeping; he is a wonderful self taught naturalist, but not only does he seem to know every species of bird, bee, wildflower and even fungus, he could also be taken for a stand-up comic. He can tell stories, true and false, and he can sing folk songs and ballads as he accompanies himself on the mandolin; the tunes become less recognisable with each intake of refreshment. Just after I had finished writing *The Wildlife of the Royal Estates* he phoned me: 'Robin, I have the very dog for you. It's got the same haircut as you – it's a little lurcher.'

He had tried to breed a dog that looked like a miniature

deerhound, and with Bramble he had succeeded perfectly. He had crossed a Norfolk lurcher, belonging to a lovely Norfolk countrywoman, Margaret Wilson, with a Bedlington terrier – an Argentinian Bedlington terrier. I took one look at the puppy and Bramble was mine. He was so small that he could fit easily into a cat basket; amazingly that was nearly seventeen years ago.

The little dog outgrew the cat basket but he remained about the same size as a poodle, or a medium-sized fox. Like all country dogs he hated foxes from the very first day he met one and he would run alongside them barking his displeasure; lurchers are supposed to run in silence, that is why the gypsies like them so much. Almost the first time I took Bramble along the road to the farm the local gypsy almost fell off his bike in admiration and offered me £25 for him.

The most exciting fox hunt was when Bramble stopped by an old pollarded willow tree and would not leave it. I thought he had smelt a duck's nest in the hollow trunk; as I looked in, the fox looked out. It shot out through the top of the tree and belly flopped into the brook before disappearing into the distance. Bramble had a problem, he hated water. This was solved by an almighty leap that took him over the brook; he too disappeared into the distance in full cry. For weeks afterwards he always stopped by the tree and looked up expectantly into the branches.

There were happy days ratting and chasing rabbits, and sad days when his amorous intentions sent him tumbling under the wheels of a passing car, as he crossed the main road with other things on his mind. He was on death's door, so I thought; the next day he was missing from his bed. I assumed he had crawled away to die; he hadn't, he was already re-crossing the main road, limping towards love.

There is no doubt that it was Bramble who got me the job as Presenter of 'One Man and His Dog'. Joy Corbett the producer came to the farm to give me a screen test, but most of the time the camera was pointed at Bramble – he passed. Each time he appeared on the screen he received fanmail. Then, with the threatened demise of the programme, it was Bramble the media wanted to photograph; and so again it was Bramble who helped to half save the old show.

At the end of one day's filming I took him to the head of the valley at Buttermere where he sat on a rock looking with wonder at the highland view – a complete contrast to our lowland landscape. Even at thirteen I walked him round Loch Muick in Scotland. The wind was so strong and cold that it whipped great spirals of water over a hundred feet into the air and then it rained – Bramble's curls disappeared and he looked like a drowned rat, but he loved every minute of it.

The final decision was a hard one. Two days earlier when I returned from a writing trip to the Cotswolds he greeted me as usual, like a long lost friend; but life just became too hard. He stumbled, he fell, he whined, he slept, the vet came and he was gone. I buried him in my favourite grass meadow, close to a sprawling ancient hedge, where I shall join him one day. The may was just bursting into flower, and as I dug, with tears rolling down my cheeks, willow warblers, skylarks and blackcaps sang. On my living room wall I have a perfect portrait of Bramble painted by Gordon Beningfield. With a strange twist of fate Bramble died on the first anniversary of Gordon Beningfield's untimely death. One chapter has really ended and a new one begins.

57

A Countryman's Millennium Who's Who

Tony 'Bomber' Blair – Britain's youngest Prime Minister for many years. His knowledge and demeanour confirm that nobody should be allowed into Parliament under the age of forty and until they have done a proper job.

He is the living personification of the 'emperor's new clothes'. Beneath the presentation, the sound-bites and the gimmicks there appears to be nothing apart from intellectual and moral nakedness.

Bomber has trodden the well worn path into public life – public school, Oxbridge, London politics and a safe seat in a far flung outpost of the country that he visits occasionally. This in current political circles is known as 'democracy'.

He is a total Europhile who seems to want to become the first Emperor of Europe. Others who have had the same dream include Nero, Hitler and Mrs Robinson from Bullock's End. His greatest claim to fame is that he was one of a group of 'leaders' who agreed to bomb Belgrade. It was the first time that Belgrade had been bombed since it was attacked by Adolph Hitler. Needless to say Bomber Blair's decision was taken in Berlin. His knowledge of, and interest in, the British countryside appear to be evenly matched – nil.

William 'Personality' Hague – Britain's youngest leader of the Opposition for many years. His knowledge and demeanour confirm that nobody should be allowed into Parliament under the age of forty and until they have done a proper job. His interests and political views are unknown.

Robin 'Quasimodo' Cook – Britain's Foreign Secretary. It is not known whether Mr Cook has been eating genetically modified foods or whether he has had en ego enlargement operation that went sadly wrong. Whatever caused his problem it is hoped that he refrains from appearing on television before the 9 pm watershed. He is the originator of Britain's 'ethical foreign policy', spelled 'b o m b s a w a y'.

Jack Cunningham – a qualified doctor, what in I have no idea. His home is in the North-East and his father was a friend of that nice man Mr Poulson. As Secretary of State for Agriculture he proved the biggest disaster since Eric the Viking. Under his reign in agriculture, farm incomes plummeted; farm suicides increased. Known in some sections of the media as 'Junket Jack'.

Gay – a word meaning happy and joyful. If I have understood things correctly the present Cabinet contains several people who are happy and joyful.

Nick 'Gay Wellies' Brown – a man who apparently owns a pair of wellington boots that are happy and joyful. Yet another politician from the North-East, currently he is Secretary of State for Agriculture; before his elevation his knowledge of, and interest in, the countryside matched those of Mr Blair.

Baroness Jay – the Leader of the Lords. A woman passionately opposed to the principles of heredity and privilege. Her father was a former Prime Minister; her ex-husband was formerly Britain's ambassador to the United States.

Ron Davies – the former Secretary of State for Wales who fell foul, or even fowl, on Clapham Common – nobody seems to know. Whatever happened on that day Mr Davies has blamed it on his 'genes', or should that be 'jeans'? I do apologise for any confusion; I am just a simple country boy doing my best.

A policeman – a man who when last seen wore a distinctive

uniform. His, or her, aim is to maintain law and order and catch criminals. A policeman was last seen in my village in the drought year of 1976.

Edward Heath – architect of Britain's entry into the E.E. (Evil Empire), also known as the E.U. (Evil Union). A great supporter of the Euro: Britain's supporters of the Euro are known as Euronators, thus making Edward Heath Britain's Euronator in chief.

The Common Agricultural Policy (CAP) – a unique system based on bluff and deception which hopes to see the destruction of rural culture and traditional farming across Europe.

CAP Reform – a fantasy enjoyed by all those people who refuse to see reality.

Supermarket – an institution designed to make a few people rich and the farming community poor.

'One Man and His Dog' – the greatest programme ever to have been on television. Threatened with extinction by the BBC.

BBC – take your pick – Ban Border Collies, the Brussels Broadcasting Corporation, Ban the British Countryside, the Brussels/Blair Corporation, The Bimbo Broadcasting Corporation, etc.